ON WINGS TO WAR:

Teresa James, Aviator

To Robert,
a fellow p...
With warme...
Jan ...
July 2,

ON WINGS
TO WAR:

Teresa James, Aviator

Jan Churchill

Sunflower University Press®
1531 Yuma (Box 1009), Manhattan, Kansas 66502-4228, USA

ISBN 0-89745-130-9

Cover:
Teresa James in front of *Ten Grand*,
the 10,000th P-47 Thunderbolt
built by Republic Aviation.

Layout by Lori L. Daniel

Contents

"If You Have Flown," by Betty Huyler Gillies   vii

Foreword   ix

Introduction   xi

Chapter 1   Mastering the Fear   1

Chapter 2   Advanced Training and Dink   20

Chapter 3   On Wings to War   31

Chapter 4   The WAFS —
                Teresa at New Castle Army Air Base   44

Chapter 5   Training at New Castle   52

Chapter 6   The Ferry Queen   76

Chapter 7   Heavy Iron   99

Chapter 8   *Ten Grand*   131

Chapter 9   D-Day Plus Forty   141

Chapter 10   Disbanded and Postwar   154

Epilogue   174

The WAFS, by Teresa James   175

Index   178

"IF YOU HAVE FLOWN"

by Betty Huyler Gillies

There are no words that can express
The Magic of that wilderness,
That wilderness away up high
Where banks of clouds float softly by
And hide the problems of earth below.
But then you know, —
If you have flown.

If you have flown, then you know
The beauty of the world below,
The meadows green, the waters sapphire blue,
You've felt that it belonged alone to you,
And as your ship obeyed your slightest will
You've felt a thrill, —
If you have flown.

For to those who sail the sky above
Comes peace of mind and understanding love,
There is no bitterness in the sky
As gently earth and clouds drift by,
All is beautiful, serene, —
You know exactly what I mean, —
If you have flown.

Teresa D. James. (Courtesy of Teresa James)

Foreword

Teresa D. James was a competent flier before she joined the Women Airforce Service Pilots. She acquired a great deal of expertise and self-confidence doing what was at that time considered a man's work. The high point of her career came when she was rostered to fly away from the Republic aircraft factory the 10,000th P-47 Thunderbolt, named *Ten Grand*. Shortly thereafter, however, Henry H. "Hap" Arnold, the Commanding General, declared that the U.S. Army Air Forces did not need women ferry pilots any more and had them summarily discharged from the service. Equally unfortunate, it was not until 1977 that these gallant and competent professional pilots received their proper recognition as members of the armed forces of the United States in World War II.

Teresa D. James and her story are a special part of aviation history, of women's history, and, thus, of U.S. history. We salute her as pioneer and professional.

Robin Higham
Professor of Aviation History
Kansas State University
Manhattan, Kansas

Introduction

In 1933, Teresa James soloed a Travel Air OX-5 at Wilkinsburg Airport in Pittsburgh, Pennsylvania. She was soon performing as a stunt pilot at air shows to earn money for additional flying time. In 1939, after she had earned her Transport License, she obtained her primary and secondary Instructor's ratings, the latter in a Waco UPF7.

Teresa instructed in the Pittsburgh area until receiving word that pilots were needed for the Women's Auxiliary Ferrying Squadron (WAFS), later to become the Women Airforce Service Pilots (WASP) in 1943. She was the ninth to report for duty at New Castle Army Air Base in Wilmington, Delaware, ferrying aircraft from 1942 until 1944, when General H.H. Arnold deactivated the WASP.

During the war, Teresa married an Army Air Forces pilot who was sent to Europe and later was reported missing in action. But not until her visit to France in 1984 for a reunion of "D-Day Plus Forty" pilots did she learn the details of his fate.

A lifetime member of the P-47 Thunderbolt Pilots Association, she was the pilot who flew the 10,000th P-47 Thunderbolt fighter, *Ten Grand,* away from the Long Island Republic Aviation factory production line. Afterwards she kept in touch with the pilots who flew this aircraft in combat.

After World War II, Teresa continued to instruct and was an avid air racer. She was commissioned in the U.S. Air Force Reserve and served until she retired with the rank of Major in 1976.

In 1990 she still maintained a keen interest in aviation from her home in Lake Worth, Florida, though she is no longer an active pilot.

During 1986 I spent time with Teresa James in Florida, sharing her love for aviation through the experiences of her career, recording her story as she told it to me. From this and from official sources at the Office of Air Force History, Maxwell Air Force Base, Alabama, much interesting information was tied together in a personal tale.

As a pilot, I was inspired by this remarkable woman's professional talent and skill, as well as by her unending devotion to her deceased husband, George Martin. This is about Teresa.

Jan Churchill

Chapter 1

Mastering the Fear

Teresa James got into flying by chance. Her brother Francis was a member of an aviation enthusiasts' club. One day in 1931, Francis X. James and two companions were flying from Pittsburgh to a Detroit air show. His mother, who was at the airstrip when the young men departed, said that they didn't have a very good takeoff and she feared they would meet with an accident.

Francis James' single-engine airplane, encountering stronger headwinds than expected, ran out of gas. He made a forced landing, and the plane struck a rut and nosed over. All three were seriously hurt, and Francis was hospitalized for six weeks with a bad leg injury. His sister, Teresa, however, didn't find out why the plane crashed until after she had learned to fly.

As soon as Francis got home from the hospital, he went back to the airport. Teresa thought he was crazy for still wanting to fly after he had almost been killed. Furthermore, the Wilkinsburg Airport hadn't impressed her; it was an uphill and downhill grass strip about 1,500 feet long with trees at each end.

> Boy, did I cuss him out. . . . Because he couldn't drive yet, Francis begged me to take him out to the airport, a five-minute drive from our house. I spent the time telling him how stupid he was to continue flying. I would drop him off and go back home.

She didn't mind him calling when he was ready to leave the airport, but after several such return trips, Francis suggested Teresa stay and go on some of the picnics with him and the other pilots. The pilots' girlfriends would pack a basket and six or seven would fly off to another airport, maybe 50 miles away, for a picnic, then fly home.

This never much interested Teresa until the day she met a pilot named Bill Angel. Though Francis had introduced Teresa to several of the pilots, whenever they had asked her to go flying, she had replied, "No way." But that day, as Teresa turned off Graham Boulevard and drove up the dirt road to reach the hangar, she glanced at the rolling hill and pea patch (later known as Blackridge), surrounded by trees, wires, and gulleys, and watched a silver plane land and taxi up to the gas pump.

> Out stepped my dream man. Bill was . . . handsome . . . and I went bananas.
> After we were introduced, he invited me to fly to Latrobe, where he was flying in an air show. Before I could think, I said yes and off we went. From takeoff to return landing, I was panic-stricken.

Teresa returned to the airport the following Sunday. Bill had invited her to go along with the gang. Teresa remembers:

> I was terrified of the idea, but after several Sundays watching everyone flying off to picnics at airports around the state, I relented. I didn't sleep that whole week, worrying about getting in the airplane; that's how scared I was.

Teresa was not only remembering her brother's accident, but also the time she had witnessed two persons burn to death in the crash of an Army plane near her home.

> When the time came to go with Bill and the group, I got in the plane, shaking from fear; we flew about 60 miles and I was petrified. But I was really nuts about this guy.

After her initial flight, Teresa hadn't planned to fly again, but two weeks later she went up with Bill again. After that she spent the whole summer as a passenger until Bill announced that he was going to Chicago to take a job with Capital Airlines.

Teresa thought that the world had ended. But actually, her world had just started. Harry Fogle, an instructor fresh from Parks Air College in St. Louis, suggested she learn to fly and surprise Bill when he came back from Chicago. Teresa began lessons with Harry and soloed on 3 September 1933, when she was 19 years old.

Teresa James and her flight instructor, Harry Fogle, in 1937. When Teresa took lessons with Fogle in 1933, he was a new instructor, "fresh" from Parks Air College, St. Louis, Missouri. (Courtesy of Teresa James)

I'll never forget that flight — I soloed in 4 hours and 20 minutes. It was early Sunday morning and the plane could have flown itself, it was such a still, beautiful morning. Actually, when I was taking instruction, I really didn't think I was flying the airplane. I thought the instructor was flying it. He was in the front seat saying things like get the nose down, get the wing down.

We had no brakes, and a tail skid rather than a tail wheel. You had to learn how to taxi. There was nothing in the cockpit but an oil gauge, an altimeter, and a gasoline thing bobbing up and down. That was it.

It was about 7:00 a.m. when Teresa and Harry Fogle took off, made one trip around the field, and landed. Harry got out, saying he had to look at something on the tail. He walked back, swung the airplane around, and positioned it for takeoff. He walked to the front of the plane and said to Teresa, "You're ready to go; you can fly this thing better than I can."

Teresa pushed the throttle and the OX-5 jumped in the air.

> I had a tree where I turned at 200 feet and a barn where I turned at 400 feet and so on. Well, when I got to the tree, and I was at 500 feet, I panicked. I nosed the plane down to lose altitude and it picked up speed. I remembered the pilots saying, "don't pick up speed." I made my first turn at Graham Boulevard, down past Beulah Church, and was really high when I turned final at Churchill Country Club.
>
> All this time I was beating my right leg to stop it from shaking. I had ridden with Bill when he slipped the airplane, and I must have automatically picked it up or something, because I slipped it to lose that altitude. I was so nervous my right foot kept going up and down on the rudder and I couldn't stop it — I kept hitting it.

Teresa made one landing and got out of the airplane, still shaking. As she walked away, she said, "Never again; they'll never get me in another airplane."

One of the men told her, "You realize you got up and got back down — all you need is flight time."

Teresa began to think about Bill coming home from Chicago, and decided to take more flight instruction in spite of herself.

Scary things still happened. She got lost on her first solo cross-country flight to Connellsville.

> I got off course and didn't recognize the places below me. I panicked and landed in a field. Seemed like 9,000 farmers came out of nowhere to stare at me. I said, "I'm not sure where I am," and they told me it was Johnstown.

Teresa had landed in a wheat field. To get her out, the farmers had to put the tail of the aircraft through an open gate to give her all the room possible and had to hold it in place until they got her signal. The aircraft barely cleared the wires at the other end of the field as it departed. Teresa eventually found her way back to Wilkinsburg where she was greeted by a worried Harry Fogle.

"What took you so long?" he asked. He saw the wheat wrapped around the solid wheels. "Where did you get that?"

Teresa James, 4 April 1934, in winter flying gear in front of an OX-5 Travel Air.

Teresa was uncomfortable, but confessed, "I got lost and landed in a farmer's field."

She later said,

It was in the newpapers the next day, so it's a good thing I told Harry the truth. I was still afraid to fly, long past when I had 60 hours of flight time. I remember when I got caught in a storm and somehow got home. It happened when I was on the way back to

Wilkinsburg Airport and was low on gas. It was absolutely the worst pickle I've ever been in and the worst storm I ever saw.

Teresa didn't know much about storms.

I didn't recognize it as one of those fast-moving, ten-minute storms. The aircraft was caught in severe up and down air currents. Lightning flashed. It was terrible. I thought I would never get down. And, we didn't wear parachutes. We had a bobble stick to tell us how much gas we had. I was looking at the gas stick and thinking, "Dear God, do I have enough to get back to Wilkinsburg?" After ten minutes, I didn't know where I was. Clouds swirled around the plane.

All of a sudden, there was a break in the clouds and I spotted the huge Penn Water Tower. I knew I was close to the airport.

It began to rain harder as Teresa headed the aircraft in the direction of the airport, after circling and trying to see through the blinding rainstorm.

I took a chance and set down where I thought the airport should be. When it turned out really to be there and the landing was made safely, I actually got down and kissed the ground. I felt really weak; I thought my knees would never stop shaking. It was a terrible, emotional experience. I figured I could never be that afraid again, but I was wrong.

Throughout her flying years, Teresa really never became addicted to flying.

The fear never really left me to the point where I said I can be sure I can go up there and get back down. I was always on top of flying; I was fright conscious. Some people I talked to were never afraid. Maybe I was an oddball, but I was absolutely terrified.

She remembered later sitting around with friends at Bettis Field having a couple of beers and bragging about flying. She had to take them all for a ride the next day. It was an ego thing. But she was still afraid.

However, the episode in the rainstorm served a good purpose. Teresa never got over a certain fear of flying, but she did get sufficient confidence in her ability to continue on in the air.

While this was going on, Bill Angel got married in Chicago. So he never came back, but Teresa learned to fly. After Bill had left the scene, Teresa's attraction to flying was meeting people and having fun.

The Wilkinsburg Airport hangar, 1936. (Photo E. L. Shryock, Pittsburg, Pennsylvania, courtesy of Teresa James)

At the airport, I met a couple of good looking guys, good dancers. This little thing about going on picnics Saturdays and Sundays was important.

Teresa worked as a floral designer. She was helping her parents design wedding and funeral bouquets in the family florist shop on Wood Street in Pittsburgh. The business began when her grandfather (his father was a gardener for the King of England) moved to Pittsburgh and had greenhouses on the rooftop of the Fort Pitt Hotel to keep the hotel supplied with flowers, palm trees, and decorations for dances. Teresa's mother saw possibilities of more business for weddings and holidays. She said, "Why not open a flower shop?" And she did — "cold turkey."

Teresa said,

My mom was a smart businesswoman who had a natural knack for it. She used to have flowers shipped in from California by air. They always sold.

She was a natural designer. First she taught me, and then I went to school to learn how to create originals — no copies.

Teresa had three brothers and two sisters. Francis, Jack, and Betty were also

Teresa James with her parents, October 1934, at Wilkinsburg Airport, Wilkinsburg, Pennsylvania. (Courtesy of Teresa James)

pilots. They grew up in Penn Hills in Pittsburgh, "home of the famous boiler-maker drink, a shot of whiskey with a beer chaser." There she attended St. Paul's Cathedral and went to Wilkinsburgh High School.

She had already established a reputation as a Marathon Dancer in the 1932 Motor Square Garden marathon when the pilots at the airfield, who often talked about sports, dared her to ice skate. In time, she became an avid speed racer and won the Bronze Medal at the 1934 Pennsylvania Skating Association Championship Meet at Duquesne Gardens.

But the two things Teresa most wanted to do in life were to be a ballet dancer and a piano player:

> . . . I am neither, but I did take ballet. My mother thought I would turn out to be a damn hussy — one of those stage-struck kids. And, I was really very stage struck.

In addition to her interest in the stage, tennis and bowling appealed to Teresa. But as she gradually controlled her fear, flying became the focal point of her life.

Teresa received Private License #31249 on 12 October 1934. She was soon performing as a stunt pilot at air shows to earn the money for additional flying

AIR SHOW
WILKINSBURG AIRPORT
Graham Blvd. at Wm. Penn Highway

Two Parachute Jumps
By "Cloud Buster" Langer
World Famous Parachute Jumper

AIRPLANE STUNTING EXHIBITION
By THERESA JAMES, GIRL STUNT PILOT
(Theresa James stole the show at the Air Progress Week
Show at the City-County Airport Last Saturday and Sunday)

HARRY FOGLE, THE FLYING ICEMAN and His Travelair
(Instructor of Miss James)

LITTLE GEORGIE HELLER
Flying a Waco F.

EXTRA SPECIAL
Children Under 12 Can Fly For 50c Until 2:30 P. M.

Sunday Afternoon
October 27, 1935

IN CASE OF BAD WEATHER SHOW WILL
BE HELD THE FOLLOWING SUNDAY

Air Show flyer for Teresa James' stunting exhibition, 27 October 1935. (Courtesy of Teresa James)

time. One day, air show pilot George Heller said, "You know, I fly these air shows, and I can show you how to do some things in an airplane."

Teresa answered, "Like what?"

"Spinning," George said.

It impressed me that the guys could do these things with the airplanes. I never really knew I was well coordinated — I found that out later. It was also my ego and everybody looking. I was always the center of attraction everyplace I went. And my mother, God rest her soul, she was so worried about me all the time.

I would meet George in the afternoons, after I got my license, and he would show me how to do aerobatic maneuvers. My mother used to worry about what time I would get home, so when I finished I would go and fly over the house at 300 feet and circle, pull the power off and shout, "I'll be home for dinner, so don't worry." You could do that then. You were supposed to stay 500 feet over a house, but there was no one around.

George showed Teresa how to do hammerhead stalls.

For some reason, that intrigued me. I was scared, but I knew everyone was down there watching, so I did it. George also showed me how to do spins and loops. I kept adding turns to the spins. I had no fear of spins, ever. It goes back to dancing. The guys used to warn me that I wouldn't pull out — that the spins were getting flatter. And then, all of a sudden, the nose would come up. It didn't look that way to me. Shortly after that Walter Beech told me I would kill myself, spinning like that.

Teresa caught on quickly.

When spinning, I picked out four points, . . . and we would do a couple of turns. Then George showed me how to snaproll. My favorite maneuver, though, was hammerhead stalls. I would pull that sucker up until it was almost ready to slide backwards — I loved to do that.

Not long after that Harry sold the airplane. The new owner cracked it up. They found out that the plane I had been doing snaprolls in had spars tied together with piano wire. Had I known that, I would have died of fright, right up there in the sky. But at that time, I could really never see the danger. That came later. When I started going to the air races in Cleveland, I remember

Teresa flew
many passen-
gers dressed
like this at Wilk-
insburg Airport,
Wilkinsburg,
Pennsylvania.

Jimmy Doolittle going around the pylons and coming across the
finish line at 300 mph. My God, to me that was terrific. I picked up
different things from different people. If they could do it, I could.

One time my mother said, "Sometimes I think I had a boy instead of a girl." I always flew in a dress and high-heels. I would kick the shoes off once I was inside the airplane. Lots of times I wore dresses because I would be working at the flower shop, or getting out of church, and I didn't bother to change. I liked the guys' attention. I loved it when we sat around and talked flying. I learned a lot from this ground flying.

We would stay at the airport until 12:00 or 1:00 in the morning, just talking about the planes and their engines, and about tearing the motors down. I did that one winter with one of the guys. He took an engine to his garage and we took it apart and put it back together again. At least I knew how that engine worked. Another good thing about flying was that I could relate to student pilots who were afraid.

Teresa wore dresses until she found out some of the guys were wearing boots and breeches for flying suits.

I thought they were real snazzy, so I got some riding breeches. Somebody once asked me if I rode horses? I said, "No, just horsepower."

Before she began her solo air show act, the "Flying Falcons" wanted Teresa to join them. This was a group that gave stunting exhibitions around the country. But they said Teresa would have to wear a parachute:

It really wasn't mandatory. I never used a parachute all the time I was stunting. Never until I went to the Roosevelt School of Aviation.

The fact that Harry Fogle never used a chute had influenced Teresa.

She started performing in air shows in 1935 at the age of 21, wearing an all-white helmet and usually flying a blue airplane. She whipped her aged OX-5 Travel Air biplane through all sorts of maneuvers during her first show at the Wilkinsburg Airport. It was her chance to make good before a big audience, performing spins and loops.

I had stars in my eyes when I saw that $50 a performance. That was big bucks in those days.

It wasn't long before the lady pilot was in demand at air shows where sometimes she was paid $200 a performance. Her specialty was doing a 26-

Teresa James (thought to have been taken at Clarion, Pennsylvania). (Courtesy of Teresa James)

turn spin from 2 miles above the earth, keeping spectators in suspense until she pulled out about 1,000 feet above the ground.

Teresa James as she just finished flying passengers for seven hours at Clarion, Pennsylvania. (Courtesy of Teresa James)

I used to leave a crowd spellbound when I'd push the throttle forward and do 26 (or more, depending on the ceiling) spinning, plummeting turns followed by 12 or more consecutive loops and then snaprolls.

Other pilots still told me that the OX-5 was flattening out. I never had trouble getting it out. I used to trim that baby tail-heavy — it spun beautifully; I could count my turns. I would have gone higher in order to do more turns, but I never used oxygen.

One day Teresa had a real scare. The whole cowling of her Travel Air blew open.

> It was frightening because the cowling blocked my visibility. I didn't want to pull the throttle all the way back. I somehow managed a landing. We found out that someone hadn't fastened the cowling down — there were three fasteners underneath. I was scared, and real glad to get that sucker on the ground.

Teresa gave stunt exhibitions at air shows in Pennsylvania, Ohio, and New York for three years until 1938.

> I was a slipping fool. I could put an airplane down anywhere, so I didn't bother to wear a parachute. Planes didn't have flaps in those days so slipping was the best way to hit a landing area.
>
> I remember going into Allegheny Airport for an air show. All the big names from the Cleveland Air Races were there. And then here I came with the OX-5 and no brakes. But I got it in and taxied up and parked beside the fancy racers. Those were the days of undiluted heroics, but you were known; yet with all my flying time, I never dreamed I'd get to be a part of history.

Billed as "AIRPLANE STUNTING EXHIBITION by Teresa James, Girl Stunt Pilot," she often stole the show. Teresa considered herself a landing specialist. After her solo, she went on and practiced landings through her entire flying life. Even many flying hours later she said, "I don't waste my time up in the air, I just practice landings."

One of her most memorable air shows was in celebration of Air Progress Week. Teresa was on the air show bill with Harold Neumann — the famous race pilot who had won the Thompson Trophy Race at the 1935 Cleveland National Air Races — as well as with noted skywriters Gordon Mogey and Joe Mackey, among others, and a group of military pilots under the command of Captain Corley P. McDarment, Commandant of the local Army Air Corps station. Captain McDarment planned to bring a group of military pilots to Pittsburgh over the weekend to open the show with an exhibition by the reserve pilots followed by a "dog fight" with smoke clouds.

The first day of the show was designated as "District Pilots Day" and all fliers in Western Pennsylvania were invited to attend a luncheon given by Allegheny County at the Fliers Club. The City of Pittsburgh paid for the

Souvenir ticket stub for an airplane ride at Johnston Airport, Pitcairn, Pennsylvania. (Courtesy of Teresa James)

gasoline. Teresa was billed as one of the headline attractions at the Aero Club's free air show held at the County Airport.

Sunday's show was a duplicate of Saturday's, with the addition of a static display of four Army air transports: a Douglas, a Boeing, a Stinson, and a Lockheed Electra.

Once again, in 1938, Teresa was billed as the "daring stunt flier of Pittsburgh" at a two-day show at Braebreeze Airport, sponsored by the Morrison Robinson Post of the Veterans of Foreign Wars. Show attendance made aviation history. Taking half an hour to climb to 6,000 feet in an OX-5, Teresa surpassed her usual 26 tailspins, then followed this with a series of loops in a spectacular exhibition said to be a world's record.

Teresa loved the air shows:

> It was the attention I got, the people who wanted to know all about flying. I had guys asking for rides. We charged two bucks apiece and gave them an exaggerated trip around the field. Afterwards they would wait around to talk about their flight. Flying people was where the big money was.

Once Teresa fell asleep in the OX-5 coming home from an air show.

> It was so beautiful, I got mesmerized. I woke up and thought how long have I been asleep in this aircraft? I used to feel sorry for all the people on the ground and what they were missing. I had tremendous trust in the Lord.

While Teresa was giving stunting exhibitions and hauling parachute jumpers to build up time for her commercial license, Harry Fogle checked her out in the front seat of an OX-5 so that she could help out with student instruction

Teresa James at the County Airport, Pittsburgh, Pennsylvania, with the U.S. Mail, 1938. (Courtesy of Teresa James)

At Wilkinsburg's first and last airmail flight, 1938, Postal Superintendent Baker of the Wilkinsburg Post Office, swearing in the nation's only female airmail pilot, Teresa James. William P. Yocum presents a bouquet to Teresa. Behind them is a Federal Guardian of the mail.

at Johnston Airport, an 1,800-foot strip on top of a hill in Pitcairn, Pennsylvania. In those days the instructor sat in front and the student in back because the planes had to be soloed from the back seat.

Actually, Teresa was instructing before she had her instructor's rating. She taught her sister Betty to fly, the fourth member of the family to qualify as a pilot. Her younger brother, Jack, eventually became a bomber pilot in World War II. And another sister, Catherine, started flight lessons but fell in love, and marriage put a stop to them. However, speaking for herself and Betty, Teresa said, "We're not going to let romance interfere with our flying the way it did with Catherine's. To tell the truth, flying and romance get along right well together."

There were a number of young men working at the nearby Westinghouse plant wanting to learn how to fly. George L. "Dink" Martin was one of them. He became an apt student, and during the next few years, Teresa would occasionally check him out on aerial maneuvers.

She not only hauled parachute jumpers in 1938 and 1939, but was also chosen to fly the U.S. Mail. National Mail Week was from 15 to 21 May in celebration of the 20th anniversary of American airmail. Teresa was selected as the pilot to carry the mail on "Pick-Up-Day," 19 May 1938, from Wilkinsburg to Bettis Field in Dravosburg, Pennsylvania. Bettis Field in the 1930s was well known as the "Gateway to the West." Roscoe Turner barnstormed many times into Bettis Field, flying a French Breguet, one of the planes left over from World War I. Turner also used to show up in his big Sikorsky biplane powered with two Liberty engines. The plane was the first built by Sikorsky in this country and was used as a German bomber in the motion picture *Hell's Angels.*

To fly the mail, Teresa had to sign two waivers, witnessed by two citizens, and take an Oath of Allegiance to the United States before a qualified official.

Her first airmail flight was arranged by Nathan M. McDowell, then a well-known stamp collector. In a ceremony at the airport prior to her 2:00 p.m. departure, McDowell pointed out that the letters bearing a Wilkinsburg cachet of the Chamber of Commerce would be valuable to philatelists. A special airmail stamp designed by philatelist President Roosevelt was used. Stamps cost 6 cents, and many Wilkinsburg residents sent letters to themselves to commemorate not only the event, but the fact that this was one of the last flights to depart from this airport, which was slated to close the following month to become a real estate development.

The fall of 1938 saw Teresa responsible for saving the lives of two Army men lost in thick, early-morning fog near her township. Using Army signals and a flapping white sheet, she flagged them to a rough, but safe, landing in a field across the street from the James' home. Though their Aeronca overturned on landing, the pilots, Roy Confer and William Loker, were unhurt.

Chapter 2

Advanced Training and Dink

By 1939 Teresa had earned enough money from air shows to go to Buffalo Aeronautical Institute in New York to work on her Primary Instructor's Rating.

> I was the only female there. I attended Ground School every day prior to going up for my flying lesson. The guys weren't too friendly. They would sit around in groups discussing flying, but they never included me. I knew I had to study twice as hard. Every night I would study the positions of the ailerons, rudder, and elevator in the maneuvers I had to practice the next day. I made a comment one day to my instructor, Charles Cox, that the brand-new Aeronca I was flying had a smell that made my stomach squeamish. He replied, "We ought to spray it with some Channel No. 5." I noticed, though, over the next several days some of the guys got sick. I just snickered.

Teresa was the first female flight instructor to graduate from Buffalo Aeronautical Institute when she received her Primary Instructor Rating on 15 July 1940, and one of only two in the country at the time. It was a tough course, but Teresa said,

> Come graduation day, it was no big deal. With the feeling of

Teresa James in 1939 at Wilkinsburg Airport, Wilkinsburg, Pennsylvania, going up for a stunting exhibition. (Courtesy of Teresa James)

being a virtuoso, I had no trouble skimming right through it. The next day I had twenty students lined up.

Doc Marsden, who managed Buffalo Aeronautical, asked Teresa after graduation to have a picture taken with him for the newspaper.

He sure built up my confidence.

During the time she was taking instruction in Buffalo, Teresa would sometimes stand behind a fence, erected so that no one could get in, and watch a strange airplane take off and land.

I didn't know what it was. I saw a low-wing job, coming in fast. I was not used to that kind of speed on final approach. There were long, finger-width pieces of wood on the wing tips and rudders, and a camera on the vertical fin, recording the action of the pieces of wood on the airframe. The pilot really slammed it in. I never dreamed that this was the P-39 and that later I would be flying it in the service.

Teresa flying back to Chicago, ca. 1939.

By age 27, Teresa had over 600 hours, earning her Commercial Transport License on 27 October 1941, presented to her at the County Airport. Teresa went to instruct at Allegheny Airport, near Pittsburgh, when it was a brand-new field. The operator told her, "We're starting out with 20 students who're coal miners up in the valley."

Teresa instructed them in an E-2 (a 40 hp Cub):

> I had two students out of twenty who I knew would make [good] pilots, and they did. They joined the Army Air Forces.
>
> The guys who were good dancers made good pilots. They had lots of coordination and were light on the controls. Invariably, I would ask a student when I took him up, "Do you dance?" If they said yes, I knew I would have a good student.
>
> I really loved flying, but I wasn't addicted to it like some people. An addiction to me would be if you took flying over something else. I enjoyed flying, and I enjoyed dancing. And I enjoyed instructing flying, maybe because there was money in it.
>
> I would do lots of talking to my students, before we flew; and afterwards, when we would sit on the ground, I would talk to them again. I only ever had three students I couldn't solo. I gained the confidence of all my students. Some were ashamed to talk to an instructor about their fears. So, I'd say, "If I could do it, you can do it." I learned to be a good pilot from flight instructing.
>
> I always wanted to race, so I would ask other pilots, "Would you consider a female racing your airplane?" [One time I guess] I asked the wrong question, because all of a sudden it was quiet. One man said, "You don't have enough money to rent this thing."
>
> I couldn't race my Travel Air, so I did ask around. How silly I was.
>
> We would have landing contests. At our home field, we would race to see who could take off and go around and land the fastest. I held the record. One windy day I headed into the wind and the airplane stopped in mid-air, it was blowing so hard. I didn't use the 1,800-foot length of the field. I just stood on the brakes, added full power, and shot off.
>
> I was around in one minute and five seconds. That was crazy. I wouldn't let my students do things like that.
>
> I did gain a lot of confidence in my ability, but I was really never sure. I thought about Amelia Earhart and her flying so far. And, I read about all the women who went down in the drink prior to Amelia. The only other woman I knew who flew was Helen Richey. She flew for Penn Central Airline, owned by Clifford Ball.

At the end of a day's flying, most of the pilots would spend evenings sitting around the airport, hangar flying and making small talk. Teresa would spend a couple of nights a week with the gang, but other nights she dated, spending time bowling and ice and roller skating. In addition to being a capable and enthusiastic pilot, Teresa was an attractive young woman with lovely dark eyes and black hair.

Teresa wasn't aware of George "Dink" Martin's interest in her until 1940. One day a sudden summer storm curtailed flying activities. Teresa remembers:

> He invited me to lunch at his house and during the ten-minute drive there, he told me his father's monument business was located in front of his home. He and his two brothers helped his Dad with sandblasting and engraving and installing headstones in cemeteries.
>
> When we pulled into the backyard of the big, old house a few blocks from the downtown area of Turtle Creek, Pennsylvania, it was like stepping into an old-fashioned flower garden. We entered the back door, and sitting around a long table in the high-ceiling kitchen were his mother, father, two brothers, and three sisters. Dink introduced me while his mother made room for us at the table.
>
> Lunch turned out to be a feast of homemade bread, nut rolls, pie, fruits, and assorted home-cooked cold cuts. Mrs. Martin had learned to cook in her native Hungary, and now she spent her days in the kitchen preparing all kinds of goodies for her family and the friends they frequently brought home.

This was the beginning of Teresa's many visits to Dink's house. They sat and talked, played records, and enjoyed each other's company. Once in a while, they went to a movie. When she went to New York for an advanced flight rating, they corresponded.

Even though they became close friends, Dink kept some things to himself. Teresa recalled:

> When I met Dink, I was at the airport where they said, "This is Dink Martin." I never knew his name was George for months. I think I was down at the house when his Dad called him "George." And, I never knew Dink was captain of his high school swim team until 1984, when I was given his varsity swim letter.

During the winter of 1940-1941, Teresa wanted to get her Secondary Instructor's Rating to be able to teach advanced and inverted flying in the

Teresa James with a Davis Monoplane at Roosevelt Field, 1941. (Courtesy of Teresa James)

Army Cadet program. There were rumors of the U.S. getting involved in the war.

Teresa went to Max Rappaport at Roosevelt Field on Long Island and, again, she was the only female. Max introduced her to instructor Bill Pyhota, who looked about 18 years old. He informed her they would fly in all sorts of weather, so she would need warm flying clothes and heavy boots.

> While they were outfitting me, I was thinking about the heavy boots. The rudder required a delicate touch on some maneuvers and I wondered how you accomplished this when you wore boots. Then I told myself to quit worrying and concentrate on doing my best.

Max gave Teresa books on the types of maneuvers she would be practicing. That night she sat in her lonely room at the Huntington Hotel and tried to study. She slept fitfully due to the cold room. The next morning she reported bright and early for her first lesson.

> I got all suited up and then had to go to the bathroom. I wished that I was a man. Every guy in that alert room watched me disappear into the ladies room. Was I ever embarrassed!
>
> Shortly thereafter I walked out to the flight line in my cumbersome flying suit with my parachute hanging on my back. Bill Pyhota told me to get into the front. . . . He showed me how to thread my shoulder harness through the seat belt and fasten it securely. We wore Gosport helmets so we could hear each other. He informed me that this would just be a familiarization flight and to follow him through on the controls.
>
> We taxied out to the active runway. The cold wind blowing in my face as we took off made me wish it was summertime. We gained altitude quickly. Bill demonstrated an Immelman followed by a falling leaf, and then he announced we were going to do inverted figure "8s." The next thing I knew, we were upside down — my feet flew off the rudders and I was hanging on for dear life. I was petrified that I was going to fall out. We flew like this for what seemed like an eternity. At this point I questioned my sanity.

After they had landed and got out of the plane Bill said, "You'd better learn how to relax; place full confidence in your seat belt or you're never going to make it." He made that comment in front of several guys and Teresa took the heat.

For the next few weeks she flew every day and studied like a demon at night. The day finally came for her flight test. She had heard that the Inspector, Guiseppi Faranicci, was really tough on students. It happened that something was wrong with the plane she flew daily, and her instructor pointed this out to the Inspector. He angrily growled, "Let her fly the new one you got in this morning — if she can fly one, she should be able to fly them all."

Teresa started to get in the front seat of the airplane when the Inspector shouted, "Get in back — I'll fly the front!"

> I had never flown the ship from the back. Everything looks different. We took off and climbed to altitude. He said, "Do a snap roll to the left and one to the right." After that he shouted, "Now give me a slow roll to the left." I thought it was the best one I had ever done. Then the Inspector said, "OK, I'll take it," and he did a

slow roll to the left and one to the right. They were no great shakes, I thought. Then he said, "You're not exerting enough pressure on the stick, so do a roll to the right."

I thought, "OK, this is one you'll remember." I popped that control stick so fast that his body was straining against the seat belt. I went on to complete my hour-long test.

Teresa then landed the Waco. The Inspector got out and walked into the office, never saying a word. She was standing by the plane looking dejected as her instructor walked up and asked her how she made out. When she said she didn't know, he remarked that the two previous male students that flew before her had flunked.

Just then Max Rappaport appeared at the office door and motioned Teresa to come into the office. There stood Guiseppi Faranicci holding up his pants suspenders in his hands. He glanced at Teresa and said, "Young lady, anyone who can pop the buttons on my pants at 7,000 feet deserves a ticket." She had passed. He laughed as he repeated to all the guys in the office that he had told her that she wasn't exerting enough forward pressure on the control stick as she started into a slow roll. "She darn near catapulted me out of the plane." This story traveled through aviation circles with lots of embellishments.

One evening during her stay on Long Island, Teresa went bowling with friends who were invited to roll with a mixed party of strangers. She perked up with interest upon hearing a tall young man in the group request the proprietor to send the news photographer away. It turned out her bowling companions were Franklin D. Roosevelt, Jr., and his wife.

Shortly before the U.S. got into the war, Teresa returned to Pittsburgh and taught her most important student advanced maneuvers. George L. "Dink" Martin learned his lessons well enough to become an Army flight instructor and later a bomber pilot.

At this time, Teresa helped organize a Civil Air Patrol unit at Johnston Airport. With all the talk of the U.S. getting involved in the war, it seemed everyone was learning to fly and trying to get as much flight time as possible. Teresa was instructing at two airports, flying students from sunup to sundown, and spending more evenings with the Martin family.

I dearly loved his mother and the Martin kids. They and their friends would rather stay home in "Ma's" kitchen than go out at night.

Then came Pearl Harbor. The Civil Aeronautics Administration (CAA) Inspector told Dink that his flying experience would probably qualify him for the Ferrying Division at Memphis, Tennessee. Two weeks later the Inspector

Betty James (left), Teresa's sister, and Teresa in their Civil Air Patrol uniforms, 1940. War rumors were heard at the time. (Courtesy of Teresa James)

called; Dink had been accepted.

But it was too late. Dink and his buddy, Bob Winters, had enlisted. Dink was now Private George L. Martin in the Army Air Corps Technical School at Keesler Field, Biloxi, Mississippi. When Dink went into the Army, he had 2,100 hours of flying time and had given 375 men flight instruction.

In June 1942, he was transferred to the 6th Photo Squadron at Colorado Springs while waiting for cadet training., Teresa felt rather lonely at the airport, even though she was flying long hours.

Lieutenant and Mrs. George L. Martin. (Courtesy of Teresa James)

I began to realize how much I missed Dink. I found myself visiting his Mom after a day's work at the airport.

Dink missed Teresa, too. He had only been in the Army seven months when he wrote his mother and told her he wanted Teresa to drive his Buick out to Colorado. So Teresa, her sister Betty, and Mrs. Martin left Turtle Creek and drove non-stop as far as Red Oak, Iowa — quite a drive in those days on two-lane roads. Mrs. Martin rode in the back seat. She had cooked a ham, egg bread, and nut noodles, and had packed fruit for the trip. She kept feeding Teresa and talking to her so that she wouldn't fall asleep driving. Two days later they pulled into Colorado Springs. Dink got a two-day pass and, said Teresa,

We just had a good time. He wanted to get married right away. I, being a Catholic, wanted to wait and have a church wedding when we got home. But, I finally consented.

Teresa and Betty were dressed in their Civil Air Patrol uniforms — all they had to wear at the time — as they and Mrs. Martin drove to the Base to pick up Dink. From there they drove to City Hall where Teresa and Dink were married. Private D.I. Means of the 6th Photographic Squadron was best man. Dink had said, "When we are married we won't tell anyone except Betty and Mom," but the next day the newpaper had an article, "Famous Stunt Pilot Married," so it was no longer a secret. Teresa recalls, "We had the most beautiful room in the Broadmoor Hotel."

For the next two weeks while Dink went to class, Mrs. Martin, Betty, and Teresa went sightseeing around Colorado Springs. Evenings were spent with Dink. But when he was transferred to Santa Maria for Primary training, the ladies returned to Pittsburgh.

Teresa then landed a lucrative instructor's job at Tomak Aviation Corporation in Pittsburgh. The flight school was owned by Bill Tomak, who also worked in a district mill.

Chapter 3

On Wings to War

Teresa had only been at Tomak a short time when she, and 89 other women, received the following telegram:

6 SEPTEMBER 1942

AFATC S 938 PERIOD FERRYING DIVISION AIR TRANS-PORT COMMAND IS ESTABLISHING GROUP OF WOMEN PILOTS FOR DOMESTIC FERRYING STOP NECESSARY QUALIFICATIONS ARE HIGH SCHOOL EDUCATION AGE BETWEEN TWENTY ONE AND THIRTY FIVE COMMER-CIAL LICENSE FIVE HUNDRED HOURS TWO HUNDRED HORSEPOWER RATING STOP ADVISE COMMANDING OF-FICER SECOND FERRYING GROUP FERRYING DIVISION AIR TRANSPORT COMMAND NEWCASTLE COUNTY AIR-PORT WILMINGTON DELAWARE IF YOU ARE IMME-DIATELY AVAILABLE AND CAN REPORT AT ONCE AT WILMINGTON AT YOUR OWN EXPENSE FOR INTERVIEW AND FLIGHT CHECK STOP BRING TWO LETTERS RECOM-MENDATION PROOF OF EDUCATION AND FLYING TIME STOP BAKER END =

GEORGE ARNOLD
COMMANDING GENERAL ARMY AIR FORCES.

Teresa James
just before enter-
ing military ser-
vice in 1942.

By that time Teresa had 2,254 flight hours with about 1,000 in the Piper Cub, 400 in the Travel Air, 254 in the Aeronca, 95 in the Luscombe, 55 in the Dart, 70 in the American Eagle, 245 in the Waco UPF, 115 in the Taylorcraft, 20 in the Stinson, as well as time logged in the Great Lakes, Brunner-Winkle Bird, Bull Pup, Curtiss Pusher, Monocoupe, Staggerwing Beech, Davis Monocoupe, Waco 10, and Autogyros. Her civilian commercial experience included employment by McClintock Air Service from 1935 to 1938 as a stunt pilot for exhibitions and hauling passengers; and between 1939 and 1942 she had done executive flying for Tomak Aviation at the Allegheny County Airport, Pittsburgh, at Becker Aircraft Corporation, Bettis Field, Pittsburgh, as well as at Martin Olek Shipyards and Gibbs Flying Service in San Diego, California.

When Teresa received her telegram, she looked forward to joining the new women's ferrying group:

Nancy Love, Squadron Leader of the new WAFS, was the first woman pilot to fly the P-51 Mustang fighter and the B-17 four-engine bomber.

I felt I could contribute to the war effort.

Her name had been located by Nancy Harkness Love — a well-known aviatrix and graduate of Vassar College, who would be the newly appointed

Squadron Leader — and Helen Mary Clark. They had gone through Civil Aeronautics Administration (CAA) records to locate all women pilots holding a Commercial license.

The concept of women flying for the military was not new. Amelia Earhart, the famous aviatrix who had been lost flying around the world, had proposed it in 1932. Then president of the Ninety-Nines, the International Organization of Women Pilots, she had suggested to her successor, Louise Thaden, that the Ninety-Nines develop a group. At roughly the same time, more than a decade before the U.S. entered World War II, a Women's Air Reserve had been organized with the idea that it would become the Corps Auxiliary in wartime. Called the Betsy Ross Corps, these women pilots, headed by Opal Logan Kuntz, offered their services to the Army Air Corps when Pearl Harbor was attacked, but General Arnold refused to use them. (These women had selected blue uniforms with Scottish hats.) By the time the Japanese attacked Pearl Harbor, several thousand women had licenses in the United States and a number had found an outlet for their patriotism and enthusiasm in the Civil Air Patrol, but not all were satisfied with that relatively small contribution to the war effort.

Meanwhile, the Army Air Corps' consistent response to War Department inquiries about using women pilots had been along the lines that it was "utterly unfeasible" as they were "too high strung." Furthermore, General Arnold felt that airline co-pilots should be trained as ferry pilots, and that women should be moved into the airline co-pilot seats. However, the airline public would not accept women in the cockpit, so Arnold's plan was not implemented. In September 1939, Jacqueline Cochran, who had just won the 1938 Bendix Trophy, wrote Mrs. Franklin D. Roosevelt, the President's wife, and suggested that women fliers could do much useful work behind the lines in wartime.

Jacqueline Cochran was both an expert flier and a wealthy woman. She had won her wings in 1932, had entered the Mildenhall-to-Melbourne air race from England to Australia in 1934, getting only as far as Bucharest, and had become the owner of her own cosmetics firm in 1935. She was the first woman to compete in the Bendix Air Race in the United States, which she had won in 1938.

Her husband was the multi-millionaire stockbroker, Floyd Odlum, and thus, in addition to being extremely talented, she had powerful friends and connections of her own and through her marriage. She knew what she wanted to do or wanted done and how it had to be handled, and she would pay for it, if necessary, out of her own pocket.

Eleanor Roosevelt's reply to Cochran's suggestion of using women fliers was that while she personally was sympathetic to the idea, the Air Corps was not.

Subsequently, in the fall of 1940, Nancy Love, then an active pilot working in the government, had written to General Robert Olds, Commanding General of the Ferrying Division, that women could be used for domestic ferrying as all available men would be needed to take aircraft to Britain. Again, General H. H. Arnold turned down the proposal and disapproved another, similar suggestion in August 1941 stating that "the use of women pilots serves no military purpose in a country which has adequate manpower at this time." He ignored the fact that in Britain women pilots of the Air Transport Auxiliary (ATA) were successfully delivering all types of military aircraft — from fighters to four-engine bombers — in the worst possible conditions without navigation instruments or radios. Women pilots had been serving in the British civilian pilot pool since it was formed on 1 July 1940.

In the spring of 1942, Jacqueline Cochran had recruited nine American women pilots to England to fly for the ATA on 18-month contracts (twelve more women from the U.S. joined after Cochran returned to America). Teresa James was to have been among them, but just at the critical moment, her mother had a heart attack and she could not leave. By the time the Cochran group was in full flight in Britain, the situation in the United States had changed drastically. Instead of needing 30,000 pilots as Arnold had thought in 1941, he found that the Army Air Forces would need 100,000 in 1942, and that there was a severe competition for this manpower.

On a lesser level, but more immediately relevant to Teresa James' future, was the fact that Colonel (later General) William Tunner of the Air Corps Ferrying Command, which had begun on 29 May 1941, had to find additional pilots for his routes which now snaked out to six continents, delivering military aircraft to the countries then fighting for democracy. Tunner arranged to hire civilian male pilots through the Civil Service Bureau at $300 a month and to commission them into the U.S. Army Air Forces after a three-month trial period if they proved satisfactory. But still aircraft piled up outside the factories as production swung into full stride.

Colonel Tunner had approached Nancy Love with the idea of employing a group of experienced women pilots. A talented pilot herself, Nancy felt that these women could be integrated into the Air Transport Command in noncombat roles to supplement the tasks of male pilots.

Love had learned to fly in Houghton, Michigan, earning her Private license in 1930 at the age of 16. She pioneered student flying clubs at Milton Academy (Massachusetts) and at Vassar College. While at Vassar, she had qualified for her Commercial Transport license.

After college, Love worked for the Bureau of Air Commerce as a test pilot, flying planes which contributed to the development of tricycle landing gear (used in the war on the large B-24 and B-29 bombers and on C-54 and C-69 transports). She also demonstrated the Gwinn aircar and Hammond "safety

Betty Gillies and Nancy Love with the B-17, four-engine bomber, on a ferry trip across the Atlantic to England, pictured here at Gander, Newfoundland.

planes." In addition, the Bureau had also assigned Love as one of the pilots to air-mark all principal cities.

Love later worked at an aircraft sales and charter company, delivering planes to customers in the New England states. She also flew in air races and air shows. In 1937 she placed in the Amelia Earhart Women's Open at the National Air Races.

When the war broke out, Love had accumulated 1,200 flying hours in 13 years and had 600 hp, instrument, and seaplane ratings. Before the war, she was the first woman to ferry planes to the Canadian border, where they were towed across the line in compliance with the Neutrality Act.

For a year before the Women's Auxiliary Ferrying Squadron (WAFS) was organized, Love worked as a civilian in the Air Transport Command (ATC) office. She mapped ferry flight routes for the pilots and became thoroughly familiar with Ferry Command procedures. In the early 1940s, she had commuted daily from Washington, D.C., in her Fairchild 24, to her job in the control office at the Martin bomber plant near Baltimore. She was secretary to Colonel Robert H. Baker, who started the Ferry Command at Baltimore for the B-26 bomber. She also flew regularly to Olmstead Air Base near Harrisburg, Pennsylvania.

After the WAFS was established in September 1942, Nancy Love was the first woman pilot to fly the P-51 Mustang fighter. In February 1943, she put her P-51 through its paces, while the Mustang aces of the future were still in Army Air Forces cadet school. Love was also the first woman to fly the B-17 four-engine bomber.

During the time that the military had disapproved of using women to fly the Army planes, Nancy Love had persisted with her proposal that highly qualified women pilots could be recruited to aid the Ferrying Division. When approval finally and officially came on 10 September 1942 with the signature of the Secretary of War, Henry L. Stimson, the Civil Service Bureau agreed to

WOMEN'S AUXILIARY FERRYING SQUADRON
FERRYING DIVISION-AIR TRANSPORT COMMAND

The WAFS logo and type from official stationery. (Courtesy of Teresa James)

pay the women pilots $250 per month, on a three-month trial basis. However, the idea of giving those who qualified a commission in the Armed Forces met a barricade in General Arnold's office, even though the idea was strongly supported by ATC and had been suggested by Colonel Olds of ATC in January 1942. The War Department repeatedly stressed that the whole subject of employing women to ferry planes within the continental United States was experimental. But women were clamoring to serve.

The aims of the group were defined by Nancy Love who said:

> The Squadron was formed to release men for more difficult flying jobs. At the present time, many skilled men are being used to ferry the light types of planes. With women handling these types, the men can be used to ferry more complicated aircraft to various points in this country and to war combat zones.

By light planes, Love meant PT-19 primary trainers and L-4B liaison craft. The Army, however, did not place any arbitrary limit to the kind of planes women could be permitted to fly. Major General Harold L. George, supervisor of the women pilots as Chief of the ATC, said that if the women showed they could fly four-engine bombers safely "after proper periods of training and preliminary work, I see no reason right now why they may not get the chance."

Eventually, during the years they served, the women pilots flew all the fighters, transports, and bombers in the Air Forces inventory, including the B-29.

Nancy Love was confident that when the WAFS came into being there would be little difficulty in filling the initial quota of 50, but she had a limited number from which to draw. Of the many women pilots in the entire United States, approximately 250 held a Commercial license, and of these, not more than 100 had more than 500 hours at the controls. Of these 100, 25 already had gone to England to ferry aircraft with the British ATA.

Betty Huyler Gillies of Syosset, Long Island, wife of B. Allison "Bud" Gillies, vice-president of Grumman Aircraft Engineering Corporation, was the first woman pilot to report to the Second Ferrying Group at New Castle Army Air Base where Nancy Love had been designated Squadron Leader.

Gillies had learned to fly in 1928 in an OX-5 Travel Air. She had bought a used DH-60X Moth to build up time for her Commercial and Transport license. A charter member of the Ninety-Nines, she served as president from 1939 to 1941. She married "Bud" Gillies in 1939, and they formed Gillies Aviation Corporation.

By December 1941, civilian flying was restricted, so Gillies flew as a utility pilot for Grumman. By September 1942, when she joined the WAFS, she had

1,400 flying hours and at that time was one of only a handful of women pilots with multi-engine ratings, having 180 hours in Grumman twin-engine aircraft.

Gillies was five feet, one-inch in height and had to used wooden blocks to reach the rudder pedals. It may be hard to imagine her doing the "man-sized" job of ferrying across the country the 13,000-pound P-47 Thunderbolt, capable of speeds over 400 mph, but she was the first woman to check out in that powerful fighter. Among the airplanes Gillies flew while ferrying for the military were the P-61 Black Widow night fighter and the B-17 Flying Fortress bomber. In January 1943, Gillies became Commanding Officer of the WAFS in the Second Ferrying Group at Wilmington when Nancy Love went to the Cincinnati, Ohio, headquarters of the ATC as WAFS executive on the staff of the Commanding General, Ferrying Division.

When the war ended, Gillies returned to private flying, taking a job in 1945 with the Ryan Aeronautical Company, giving instrument instruction to its test pilots. She flew the Ryan Fireball, a Navy FR-1 fighter. Gillies, like Teresa James, was also commissioned a Major in the Air Force Reserves.

After Love and Gillies, the following WAFS appointments were made in the order listed:

Cornelia Fort (killed in service)
Aline Rhonie (Brooks)
Helen Mary Clark
Catherine Slocum
Adela (Del) Scharr
Esther Nelson
Teresa James
Alma Heflin McCormick
Barbara Poole
Bernise I. Batten
Nancy Batson Crews
Kathryn Bernheim (Fine)
Delphine Bohn
Phyllis Burchfield
Barbara Donahue (Ross)
Barbara J. Erickson (London)
Betsy Ferguson (Wood)
Dorothy Fulton
Helen McGilvery
Gertrude Meserve (Tubbs)
Florene Miller (Watson)
Esther Rathfelder (Westervelt)
Helen Richards (Prosser)

The first review of WAFS, September 1942, at Wilmington. Colonel Baker and Nancy Love pass by the women. From l to r: Betty Gillies, Esther Nelson, Cornelia Fort, Teresa James, Catherine Slocum, Adela Scharr, Helen Mary Clark, and Aline Rhonie.

Dorothy Scott (killed in service)
Evelyn Sharp (killed in service)
Katherine Rawls (Thompson)
Barbara Towne (Fasken)

Aline Rhonie had been accepted by the British ATA as a ferry pilot, but decided to wait for the WAFS to be organized. She did evacuation work in 1939 for the British Women's Volunteer Service and served in France with the women's Red Cross ambulance corps. An artist of note, she did murals at Roosevelt Field, New York. Catherine Slocum was the wife of Richard W. Slocum, general manager of the *Philadelphia Evening Bulletin.*

During the time that Nancy Love was promoting the use of women pilots for military flying in the U.S., Jacqueline Cochran was in England with the American women pilots flying with the British ATA.

She returned to the U.S. in mid-September 1942, just as the formation of the WAFS was announced, and she protested vigorously that Nancy Love had been given precedence in an arrangement that she felt she had originally proposed. Washington responded diplomatically by approving two Army Air Forces programs for women. Nancy Love's group — the Women's Auxiliary Ferrying Service (WAFS) — would ferry planes for the Air Transport Command, and Jacquline Cochran's group would prepare novice pilots in the Women's Flying Training Detachment (WFTD) for eventual service in the WAFS.

While Love's group was being flight-checked and trained for almost "immediate" service, Cochran's women were training for "eventual" service.

As part of the 319th Army Air Forces Flight Training Detachment, Cochran's WFTD girls, in time, would train at Avenger Field, Sweetwater, Texas, but when her program started, they were based at Hughes Field at Houston Municipal Airport. "Aviation Enterprises," an aviation school on the grounds, provided flight training under Army supervision.

Army personnel did not welcome the women pilots. They had to report for duty at their own expense, were given no uniforms, and had to find their own lodgings. The only bright spot for the WFTD women was Cochran's welcoming speech when they checked into Houston's Rice Hotel. There was a flurry at the door as Cochran came in, followed by the flight contractors. She was neat and tailored, wearing a small silver propeller with a large rosette diamond in the center of her lapel. She leaned on a chair as she told the women, ". . . You are all experienced pilots. There isn't a girl in this room who has less than 250 hours, and most of you have more. If things don't run smoothly at first, just remember that you will have the honor and distinction of being the first women to be trained by the Army Air Forces. You are very badly needed."

Captain Paul C. Garrett gave them a different welcome, saying, "You may think you are pretty hot pilots. I'd advise you to forget it. You're here to learn to fly the way the Army flies." Garrett then administered the oath of office which made the women Civilian Student Pilots, Unclassified, 9C-1 (subject to Retirement Act) 43-W-1.

The WFTD women's routine started with getting up at dawn when they were picked up by trucks and driven to Hughes Field. Not having been issued uniforms, they were a scruffy looking group in blue jeans or whatever old clothes they had. For meals the girls marched daily to a "greasy spoon" on the airport (it was an airline catering service), and they used the public restrooms. There were no rules and regulations. Many women stayed in rooming houses. Henry Erdmann, owner of Aviation Enterprises, and Jackie Cochran hired a housemother, Mrs. Clifford "DiDi" Deaton, to look after the women. This first class had to contend with lots of inconveniences.

The aircraft they trained in were almost "basketcases" — two Aeroncas and three Taylorcrafts. There were five civilian instructors who had no more flying time than the women they were teaching. There was also a man to teach navigation and meteorology along with an Air Corps instructor for calisthenics, fondly remembered as the one "who nearly killed us all."

After the women completed Primary Training, five BT-13s arrived for basic training. They were known as the "Vultee Vibrator" and they could be tricky to fly. The civilian instructors had never seen them before, so the Army instructor pilots taught the civilian instructors to fly the aircraft, and the next day the civilians taught the women. It was a classic case of the blind leading the blind. There were a few washouts in the BT-13s.

On 5 February 1943, five new AT-6s arrived at the field — more advanced trainers with 450 hp engines. Once again, the Army instructors taught the civilian instructors who in turn checked out the women. Two months later, on 5 April, they received twin-engine trainers. These were known as the "Bamboo Bomber" because of their wooden construction. Cessna built this aircraft for the Air Corps in 1940 as the AT-8 (T-50); later hundreds were ordered as the AT-17 and UC-78, powered by two Jacobs L-4MB engines rated at 225 hp each. Once again the same training procedures were followed.

In April 1943, 22 women graduated in this first WFTD class. Cochran pinned wings on them that had "43-W-1" inscribed on the shield. Aviation Enterprises awarded each a certificate stating that she had "completed the entire curriculum as a Ferry Pilot at the 319th Army Air Forces Contract Flying School in Houston." Some of the women graduating from Sweetwater were assigned to the four Ferry Bases — Dallas, Texas; Long Beach, California; Romulus, Michigan; or New Castle, Delaware. Others were assigned to various military bases for towing targets and testing aircraft.

By May 1943, the WFTD had moved to Avenger Field in Sweetwater, Texas, a bleak and arid place known for its sweltering summers, dust storms, and remoteness. About 40 miles west of Abilene in central Texas, Sweetwater didn't have the fog problems of Houston, but it did have a constant 25 mph northerly wind blowing red dust across Avenger Field. Temperatures reached 100 degrees in April and stayed there until fall. Half of the incoming 43-W-4 class had reported to Houston, but by May the entire class was at the all female base of Avenger. Both classes and aircraft were moved from Houston to Avenger Field.

The curriculum at Houston had included 170 hours of flying, divided into three phases: primary (lightplanes — Aeroncas, Taylorcraft, Fairchild PT-19s); basic (BT-13s); and advanced (AT-6, AT-17). In addition, there were 20 hours of Link instrument trainer and 180 hours of ground school. When the program moved to Avenger Field, it was extended to 30 weeks and comprised of 70 hours for each phase of flight training. The ground school was extended to 560 hours which included 137 hours of military training and 81 hours of physical training. The attrition rate averaged 40 percent. As the war went on, women with only 35 flying hours were admitted to the program.

The women followed a strict military regimen, lived in barracks six to a room (with one bathroom in between to be shared by 12 women), marched wherever they went, did calisthenics, and ended their 16-hour long day with taps and quite exhausted. It was a strange arrangement because the administration of all the activities at the field was in the hands of an Army major assisted by an Army staff. Actually, the Army had no jurisdiction over the women because they were civilians and as such could leave any time. But these were ladies with a purpose, so they took part in parades, infantry drills, barrack inspections, and even took the same oath of allegiance as male cadets. Later the women would wear side arms when they were flying airplanes with secret military equipment.

Oversized coveralls were issued for "flight suits." The girls called them "zoot suits" because of the poor fit. After a trainee soloed in the AT-6, she wore red socks until graduation. The earlier graduating classes purchased clothes from the PX for some sort of unofficial uniform: tan general's trousers, a white short-sleeved shirt, and an officer's garrison hat.

It was not until 1944, after the WFTD joined with the WAFS to become the WASP, that the women got official uniforms.

Chapter 4

— The WAFS —
Teresa at New Castle Army Air Base

While Jacqueline Cochran was still making plans for her WFTD group to assemble in Texas, Teresa James was catching a train in Pittsburgh, bound for Wilmington on 17 September 1942. It was hard for her to believe that she would be part of a very select and experienced group of women to be ferrying planes for Uncle Sam.

Imagine it. The Spirited Women, Powder Puff Pilots, Bird Women, Sky Menaces trying to get in the Army.

She even said a little prayer:

Whereas, they have decided to let us try, be it resolved that come hell, high water, and insulting criticism, we will not let Washington down. Amen.

Teresa looked forward to joining the WAFS, and her husband, Dink, didn't mind her flying with the Army, although he kept telling her to be careful.

Teresa checked into the DuPont Hotel in downtown Wilmington. She didn't get much rest that first night and was up before dawn. The city was still asleep when she looked out the window as she jotted a few notes in her diary:

When Teresa James first arrived at New Castle Army Air Base, parachutes were issued to all ferry pilots.

A city already famous for her "Firsts" in American history. First iron sailing vessel was made here. First iron steamship. A large percentage of explosives used by the Allies in World War I were made here. And now she is about to harbor the first female ferrying squadron.

At 6:30 a.m., Teresa was to meet in the coffee shop with two other prospective WAFS, Helen Mary Clark from Englewood, New Jersey, and Aline Rhonie from New York. She hoped they would be able to give her some pointers.

After introductions, Teresa and the two women shared a taxicab to the base. Helen Mary had a quiet, charming dignity, a warm friendliness, and was a person who made Teresa feel at ease.

The next day Teresa wrote in her diary:

> Helen Mary said I had nothing at all to worry about, but I find myself afraid. My flight check is scheduled for 11:00 and I find it hard to do away with time. I hope, with fear and trembling, it will not be in that low-winged job I see in the distance. Don't know where the nose rides or anything.

On the 21st, Teresa had a check ride in a Taylorcraft L2-B with a Lieutenant Saccio. They took off and climbed to 2,500 feet, did some power stalls, 720 turns, lazy eights, chandelles, and steep turns. They returned to the field, landed, and the Lieutenant still hadn't said a word. Wondering how everything had gone, Teresa was told to go to Headquarters. It was not until Nancy Love appeared to tell her she had passed that she got the good news. But the Board still had to pass her, and she had to pass the physical.

New Castle Army Air Base was new and not what Teresa had anticipated. Buildings and roads were under construction and mud was everywhere. "I don't know what I expected, probably old red brick buildings with ivy clinging all over." Yet in a short time, the base was to become the eastern hub of the Second Ferrying Group, Ferry Division, Air Transport Command.

Teresa and the others were to live in Bachelor Officers' Quarters 14 (BOQ14), which by late September would be distinguished from the surrounding dormitories by its venetian blinds and flower gardens as well as its housemother.

Teresa noted in her dairy:

> Mrs. Anderson came to live with us. She is official housekeeper of our BOQ. She likes girls and flying. Plenty of both here. We like her too — so much that she has already been designated as "Andy." Officers Club opened. It's nice. Things are going awfully fast around here. Houses, for instance. There are lines drawn in the mud at dawn and inhabited dwellings at sunset. Roads become paved thoroughfares in the twinkling of an eye.

The 44 square-shaped rooms in BOQ14 had a bed and a dresser for each

Teresa's room in BOQ 14, Wilmington. She had a lounge chair, end tables and lamps, and a radio sent from home in Pittsburgh. She still has the RCA radio in her Florida home. Note the pine boards and tar paper. "The wind whistled through," Teresa said, "but I made it homey looking." (Courtesy of Teresa James)

resident, as well as a maple chest, a pine wardrobe, and a bright blue scatter rug. Walls were removed on each floor to provide a lounge. The first 15 WAFS pilots moved into second floor rooms. Most of the women added quilted bedspreads and curtains, as well as pictures of loved ones and aircraft, plaques and maps on the walls. Teresa's bookshelf contained the latest work by General Billy Mitchell, the deceased apostle of American air power.

Teresa remembers her first day at BOQ14. She had to walk along plank boards to get to the building which was surrounded by mud. Climbing to the second floor, she stepped into a bare, board-partitioned room.

> I was so thrilled with the prospect of flying the Air Forces' planes, I would have slept on the floor. The room was a far cry from my lovely room at home. I went in search of the bathroom and found, to my dismay, that it had open shower stalls and commodes. There were washbasins in a line 12 feet long with a pine shelf above them where you could place your soap and makeup. Several individual mirrors were placed above the pine shelving over the wash stands.

Rugs, however, were provided for the bathrooms, as a concession to femininity.

At New Castle, Teresa met Betty Gillies, "a wee person with the merriest blue eyes"; Esther Nelson, "a tall, pleasant girl who looked as if she had escaped from the pages of Vogue"; and Cornelia Fort.

Cornelia, 23, was a graduate of Sarah Lawrence College and had been instructing in a tiny Piper Cub at dawn the day the Japanese bombed Pearl Harbor. According to Teresa, early that morning of 7 December 1941, Cornelia had driven from Waikiki to the John Rodgers civilian airport right next to Pearl Harbor, where she was a civilian flight instructor. Shortly after 6:30 a.m., she began takeoff and landing practice with a regular student. Just prior to approaching for their last landing, Cornelia looked casually around and saw a military plane coming at her. She jerked the controls away from her student and jammed the throttle wide open to pull above the oncoming plane. Cornelia told Teresa,

> He passed so close under us that our celluloid windows rattled violently and I looked down to see what sort of plane it was. The painted red balls on the tops of the wings shone brightly in the sun. I looked again with utter disbelief. Honolulu was familiar with the emblem of the Rising Sun on passenger ships, but not on airplanes.
>
> I looked quickly at Pearl Harbor and my spine tingled when I saw billowing black smoke. Still I thought it might be some kind of

coincidence or maneuvers.

Then I looked away and saw the formations of silver bombers riding in. Something detached itself from an airplane and came glistening down. My eyes followed it and it exploded in the middle of the harbor. I knew the air was not the place for my little airplane so I landed as quickly as I could. A few seconds later, a shadow passed over me and simultaneously bullets spattered all around.

Suddenly that little wedge of sky above Hickam Field and Pearl Harbor was filled. We counted anxiously as our little civilian planes came flying home to roost. Two never came back. They were washed ashore weeks later on the windward side of the island, bullet-riddled. Not a pretty way for the brave little yellow Cubs and their pilots to go down to death.

After getting back on the ground with her student, Teresa said that Cornelia discovered a couple of bullet holes in the right wing of their Piper Cub. She stayed on the island another three months, then returned to the United States by convoy. None of the pilots wanted to leave, but there was no civilian flying in the island after the attack. Cornelia and the other pilots each felt they had a score to settle with the Japanese, who had brought murder and destruction to their islands. The only way Cornelia could fly was to instruct in the Civilian Pilot Training Programs.

Weeks passed, then Cornelia received a telegram like Teresa's; immediately she made plans to report to New Castle Army Air Base.

Teresa made a few more notes in her diary that same day of her check ride:

THINGS I BET I NEVER FORGET:

Astonishment at the sunlight peeking through cracks of my room in the BOQ, the sagging of the cot and the sheer discomfort of the one iron chair. [Later, Teresa fixed up her corner room on the second floor of BOQ14 — the girls called it the "Waldorf Astoria."]

Sensation of sitting on one side of a closed door while your destiny is being tossed about on the other side. . . .

Relief when Colonel Baker said I was accepted for training. . . .

Friendliness I saw registered in Adela Scharr's large eyes.

That afternoon, three hours were spent at the Sub-Depot drawing equipment: flying jacket, helmet, goggles, boots, coveralls.

Teresa wrote in her diary:

I never was sure of my size. In case the great poet who wrote of

Teresa James arriving at New Castle Army Air Base for her first flight check in an L2-B.

the famous 600 had been writing of us, he could have started thus:

Into the intial training period
flew the ill-fitted squadron.

I look forward to knowing these girls better. From all appear-
ences and conversations, I do not have my doubts. What a day!
Eleven years ago on this date a bomb exploded in Manchuria and
gave the Japs an excuse to go a warring. . . .
Regular school session starts tomorrow.

By 8:30 p.m. the day of the check ride, Teresa was dead tired when she
made a few additonal notes in her diary:

Strange what a lamp or two, curtains and rug will do to a room
— even this room. The fellows moved out of this building very
reluctantly, I understand. We are used to the masculine attitude
toward women and aviation, thank goodness. Funny about men.
They even speculate when they see a woman back into a parking
space in an automobile. If she does a good job, they swear it was
luck or an accident. I wonder how they will eventually react to us.
There is no such thing as flying day in and day out by luck or
accident.

Chapter 5

Training at New Castle

Orientation classes at New Castle began at 8:00 on 21 September 1942. By 24 October there were 20 WAFS; they straggled in during the rest of the year and the Squadron was complete by January 1943. The original group of 25 WAFS came from 14 states. Twelve were married and ten were college graduates. Their average flying time was 1,162 hours (ranging from 532 to 2,627). Five owned their own airplanes, which they had flown all over the United States. They all had been flight instructors. Nancy Love, a tall, gracious blonde, still in her twenties, stressed that the WAFS was a group of *actual flying pilots* and that there would be no ground personnel except for some top administrative officials. Love's office was a simple, unadorned room whose three doors, leading to other offices, were wide open. People could walk through at will. When, in later months, she spoke with the press about the "girls," there was always a seriousness in her voice, as though she never forgot for a moment the hard, grueling, and often dangerous job they were being called to do. She asked reporters not to play up the glamour side.

Four weeks of classes followed orientation, covering navigation, meteorology, military courtesy, military law, Morse code, and close-order drill. Lieutenant Richard H. Jordan was the WAFS ground instructor. The women were familiarized with guard duty, rifles, and a .45 pistol. The schooling was to acquaint them with the Army's way of doing things. Much of the classroom time had to be devoted to instructions regarding filling out Army forms.

When the full complement of WAFS was on the base, it was divided into two groups. The first rose at 7:00 a.m. and finished the work day at 5:00 p.m.;

the second began and ended its day one hour later. One group would study and do classroom work in the morning and fly in the afternoon; the other simply reversed this schedule.

During the training period, the WAFS were given regular government-issue flying suits. On the shoulder of the left side of the flying suit was the insignia of the Army Air Forces Air Transport Command (AFATC). The design was similar to that of the old Ferrying Command with the Morse code changed to indicate the initials of the AFATC. The insignia of the AFATC was silver; that of the Ferrying Command was gold.

When training was over and the women actually started flying operations, they wore their own uniform which they ordered in Wilmington and paid for themselves. The uniform was a symbol of their right to wear pilot wings.

Nancy Love had chosen the material to be used. The tailor put pleats in front in case anyone had a large stomach, but he didn't know much about women, because the pleats accentuated any extra weight. Teresa remembers going to Carlson's Tailor Shop and being measured by Mr. Carlson himself.

> We were standing up and Mr. Carlson was on his knees. He measured outside and instead of coming around with the tape to measure the inseam, he just looked. He guessed the inseam measurement, as he was too embarassed to touch a lady to measure the inseam length. So we ended up with baggy pants and had to take them to be refitted.

The WAFS adopted a uniform consisting of a short gray-green gabardine jacket with a collar and pockets and trimmed with buttons. Its detached belt had a cloth-covered plastic belt buckle similar to that worn by Army Air Forces officers. It could be worn with either slacks or skirt, tan shirt open at the neck, and an overseas cap. For dress wear, a white shirt was used, also open at the neck. The command insignia, a modernistic design of an airplane flying across the top of the world, was placed over the left breast pocket.

Gold wings, like those of the Civilian Air Transport Command, were placed over the upper left-hand pocket of the gabardine jacket as well. The letters ACFC on the wings stood for Air Corps Ferrying Command. The wings had been designed before the Air Corps and the Ferrying Command had become the Army Air Forces in May 1941, and before the Ferrying Command had become the Air Transport Command on 9 March 1942.

On the left sleeve of the jacket, the WAFS wore the insignia of the Army Air Forces, a blue disc with yellow wings and a white star with a red center. Beneath this insignia were the letters WAFS. The wings and the propeller blade worn on the jacket lapel and cap were the insignia of the Army Air Forces and aviation cadets.

Teresa James in her original WAFS uniform (now in The Smithsonian Institution, display #5756, 1977-1028-1032), in November 1942.

The WAFS liked their uniforms so much that when Jacqueline Cochran later designed a blue uniform after the organization became the WASP in

August 1943, some of the women said they would resign before they gave up their "grays."

On ferrying trips, the women wore just a shirt and slacks or GI cold-weather flying suits (fur-lined leather known as "monkey" suits), leather jackets, and, of course, parachutes, leather helmets, silk scarfs (made from old parachutes), goggles (for open-cockpit aircraft), and headsets. In the winter, the flying clothes and parachutes weighed about 30 pounds. Each woman was issued her own parachute for the duration. She was personally responsible for having it examined every 10 days and opened and repacked every 60 days. Portable oxygen equipment was not carried because, as domestic ferry pilots, the women seldom flew above 12,000 feet.

After delivering aircraft, the WAFS usually wore their regulation jackets and skirts on the return trips to their bases. Their schedule was irregular because of weather problems and distances between delivery points. Often weeks would pass before a full squadron was "all present" at the base. The women weren't allowed to hitch a ride home on military aircraft, so they had to travel on public train, bus, or plane, unless they could be assigned an aircraft to fly back, and they often were mistaken for airline stewardesses.

Teresa recalled a time when it rained for six days and the women couldn't fly, so time was spent on ground school and drill. Lieutenant Jordan was a patient drillmaster; Captain Onas P. Matz was Operations Officer. More new recruits arrived from every section of the country. Helen Richards from Boise, Idaho; Barbara Poole from Detroit; Gertrude Meserve from Boston; Barbara Erickson from Seattle; Florene Miller and Delphine Bohn from Texas; and Phyllis Burchfield from Pennsylvania. All were put through the same checks and flight tests.

The weather finally improved. Teresa sat in the Alert Room listening to Nancy Love, Commander of the WAFS, give her pilots their orders for the day. The women sat on folding chairs, desktops, and the floor, with a gray-green locker for a backrest. Their flying suits were rumpled. Little Betty Gillies had a broad seam around her minute waist, where a careful tailor had taken a tuck so that she wouldn't drown in her borrowed coveralls.

One by one, the women's names were called. So many minutes of dual for the tall, slim blonde whose hair curled all over her tousled head; solo for the brunette with the big, dark eyes. So many hours of drill for the week ahead, and classroom at a definite time each day.

When Mrs. Love concluded her orders, the women straggled out into the sunshine. Those flying walked over to the Taylorcraft on the line, along with their Army check-pilots. The other women stood around, leaning against the building, or used their parachutes for cushions while they did some hangar flying until their turns came. Traffic patterns, Army style, were drawn in the dust and soft-voiced comments moved intently back and forth.

Esther Nelson, an interior decorator in civilian life, at New Castle Army Air Base in 1942.

The women took the training very seriously even though they all were experienced pilots, some with more flight time than their instructors. They knew they were guinea pigs — that the standards they set would determine whether or not their chiefs continued to use women for ferry work. They knew how much depended on them, and they were keenly aware of their responsibility and proud of it.

Over in England, American women were doing a superb job of ferrying Spitfires, Hurricanes, and Wellingtons, but thus far the WAFS only had light trainers entrusted to them. This didn't dampen their enthusiasm, however. "Just give us time," seemed to be the unspoken comment. "Give us time and we'll prove ourselves."

Like other WAFS, Teresa spent nearly all her waking hours in uniform. She was always on call, so there was little sense in wearing civilian clothes. When one squadron went to Dallas, three weeks passed before anyone saw a single

The women's first appearance in complete WAFS uniforms, 1943, probably in Baltimore, Maryland. From l to r: Helen Mary Clark, Nancy Batson, Helen McGilvery, Teresa James, Gertrude Meserve, Esther Nelson, Betty Gillies, and Dorothy Fulton.

The Alert Room, NCAAB. Teresa James recalls, "This is where we waited when the weather was stinking. One day one of the girls was resting on the sofa with a zipper undone. The CO came in, and although he didn't comment, the next day a directive was issued that we "stay fully clothed." On sofa, Nancy Battson and Liz Lundy; at table, Gertrude Tubbs and Ruth Adams in foreground; Teresa James in right in back of room.

woman pilot out of uniform. Then one night there was a dance at the Officers Club and the women went all out for the occasion. They wore long evening dresses, with flowers pinned to the shoulders, and fixed their hair into evening coiffures. When they arrived at the party, no one recognized them.

The women, with their Civil Service status, received $3,000 per year, and $6 per diem when on ferrying trips. After completion of their initial schooling, they only spent about 10 percent of their time at New Castle. While on ferry trips, they usually stayed in hotels, as few military bases had quarters for females, though occasionally a room could be had in the nurses' quarters. They had to pay 50 to 75 cents a day for their rooms on base, depending on whether the quarters were single or double. They could pay by the month, but they still had to carry some kind of coin purse with them daily. Over at the Officers Mess, they had to pay the cashier for each meal. The Mess, a temporary arrangement, looked more like a summer camp dining-room. Long wooden tables with attached benches occupied the center of the room with an old-fashioned pot-bellied, coal-burning stove at each end. The WAFS pilots, along with officers and visiting civilians, gave their orders for the simple, wholesome food to an enlisted soldier-waiter.

Physical fitness was no problem for the WAFS as a lot of plain, ordinary walking was necessary each day to get around the base. The flying field and hangar were a good distance from the barracks and mess hall. The WAFS classroom was a quarter mile from everything else on a route that went past the enlisted men's barracks and the post guardhouse.

The WAFS Alert Room was located in one of the hangars. It was a rather barren place in which the women waited for flight assignments, whiling away the time playing cards or reading. A pegboard on the wall, with colored golf tees for pegs, showed where every WAFS pilot was at that particular moment.

On base, Teresa was either in school or in the Ready Room. School was always in session at ferry bases, and pilots, when not flying, were expected to attend to keep current on such subjects as meteorology, navigation, and new flight techniques. As the war progressed, WAFS were given instrument training for bad weather flight. Some bases, such as New Castle, had Link trainers, an enclosed aircraft cockpit, complete with all aircraft instruments. The trainer moved on a fixed platform and simulated flight so that pilots could learn to fly solely by reference to instruments — the only way they could fly if they inadvertently got into clouds. The pilots were supposed to use visual reference in good weather, but conditions could change rapidly and unexpectedly.

In the 1940s, weather stations were few and far between and forecasting was rather primitive. The "Maytag Messerschmitt training," as it was called at New Castle, was valuable for all types of weather conditions, as these could be simulated in the safety trainer. There were many pilots who, with only Link

Teresa James received her Instrument Rating almost two years after joining the WAFS. Her certificate shows a date of 1 July 1944.

FERRYING DIVISION Air Transport Command

Be it known that

WASP THERESA D. JAMES

HAS SATISFACTORILY COMPLETED THE COURSE OF

INSTRUMENT TRAINING --- AAF Reg. 50-3.

Given at ...

HEADQUARTERS, 555TH AAF BASE UNIT, 5TH FERRYING GROUP,

COMMAND

FERRYING DIVISION AIR TRANSPORT COMMAND LOVE FIELD,

DALLAS, TEXAS.

RUSSELL H. MINSON, Lt. Col. AC

Date

1 JULY 44

trainer instruction, managed to beat Old Man Weather when caught in instrument meteorological conditions.

In those days, there were two types of instrument ratings. Holders of a white card could fly instruments to shoot an approach, whereas holders of a green card could only fly Instrument Flight Rules (IFR) en route and make a fairly slow descent to 2,500 feet above the ground. Below that altitude, they had to have visual flight conditions.

Teresa James received her instrument rating in 1944 in a Douglas C-47. Other women were able to get ten hours in the Lockeed A-34 twin-engine Ventura bomber. Teresa recalled,

> At that time, we didn't have to do much on instruments — just things like engine-out procedures and recovery from stalls, and how to fly the radio-range courses [RADIO-RANGE — RADAR]. You had to have both ears cocked when you flew that thing where you matched up the sounds of the dahdits to know your position. And, you had to depend on the old fan markers. All our ferrying was supposed to be VFR [Visual Flight Rules], but we had to have our instrument ratings just in case we got caught in instrument conditions. We didn't just go out and fly IFR; in fact, the male pilots didn't either. It was just an extra precaution.

Women ferry pilots had little or no private life. They worked 50 to 60 hours a week or longer. One woman spent only four nights at her home base in six weeks. The shapeless canvas B-4 bags assigned to all ferry pilots, of coat length when unzipped, with huge patch pockets on each side, had to be packed at all times, so that the pilots could leave on a moment's notice. There was little time between flights, and there were no days off. The women wouldn't have taken them if there were. They would much rather stay on base than miss a flying assignment. Like male pilots, they would rather fly than eat.

In January 1943, Nancy Love was transferred from Wilmington to Ferrying Division Headquarters in Cincinnati, and from there she organized three more WAFS squadrons at Long Beach AAB, California, Romulus AAB, Michigan, and Dallas AAB, Texas. Five WAFS from the original group at Wilmington were transfered to each of these squadrons to form a nucleus.

For her pilots, Love planned the housing, transition at pursuit schools, and ferrying assignments. Betty Gillies was CO at New Castle, Barbara J. Erickson (London) at Long Beach, Barbara Donahue (Ross) at Romulus, and Delphine Bohn at Love Field, Dallas. The Flight Squadrons, under the Commanding Officer, worked along with the men of the Ferry Command on an equal footing. They qualified through the same ground school classes as the men, and every Saturday they marched with them during the Base Review.

Teresa James was Flight Leader for this group of PT-17s (Boeing Stearman). L to r: Katherine Rawls Thompson (Olympic Swimming Champion), Phyllis Burchfield, Nancy Batson, Delphine Bohn, Florene Miller, and Teresa James at Sheppard Field, Wichita Falls, Texas, in December 1942.

Getting ready to ferry a UC-61, a four-place Fairchild, from the factory at Hagerstown, Maryland, are Helen McGilvery, Teresa James, Dorothy Fulton, Dick DuPuy, Sis Bernheim, Gertrude Tubbs, Betty Gillies, and Nancy Love, 1942.

Barbara Erickson at Long Beach was an extremely active CO, flying every mission possible. Without giving any thought to the time involved, she once flew four 2,000-mile flights in three different types of aircraft in a five-day time period. This made her eligible for the Air Forces Medal. At a special ceremony, General Arnold presented her with a Citation, signed by President Franklin D. Roosevelt, and the medal.

WAFS 14 — actually the thirteenth girl to report to the original group, as there was no number 13 — was Gertrude Meserve Tubbs, who had learned to fly at Boston in a Piper Cub. Gertrude was dedicated to flying; when the war came along and no civilian flying was allowed along the East Coast, she went inland to Orange, Massachusetts. When she received the September 1942 telegram from General Arnold, she had enough hours but no 200 hp rating, so she went to Concord, New Hampshire, to fulfill that requirement in a Cessna 145. With that accomplished, Gertrude reported to New Castle AAB as WAFS 14. She noted,

> I was a little country girl flying a plane with a star. I always dreamed of flying military aircraft, but never thought I really would.

Katherine Rawls, another WAFS pilot, was a champion swimmer and had been a member of three Olympic teams, excelling in diving. In 1937, she had won four individual titles as National Swimming Champion. She had learned to fly at her husband's flight school. When the Navy took over the airport, her husband, Captain Theodore H. Rawls, joined the RAF Ferry Command, while Katherine joined the WAFS.

The Air Transport Command was anxious to qualify as many WAFS pilots as possible on pursuit (fighter) planes so that they could handle all the pursuit ferrying. As the production of trainers and liaison-type aircraft began to taper off, the production of combat aircraft increased. Losses were heavy in both the Pacific and European theaters. A Pursuit School was established at Palm Springs, California, and subsequently at Brownsville, Texas. ATC did not want men side-tracked on ferrying pursuit planes because single-engine, or even twin-engine, pursuit was not of value in the course of training men for overseas four-engine transport and bomber deliveries.

The WAFS initially interviewed and hired its own pilots, until 26 January 1943, when Colonel Tunner received a message from General Arnold's office directing that henceforth the Division could employ only those women who had graduated from Jacqueline Cochran's Women's Flying Training Detachment in Texas. This was a great blow because the first graduates from WFTD would not be available until May, almost four months away, a matter of great concern due to the pilot shortage.

Gertrude Meserve Tubbs, WAFS 14 — actually the thirteenth woman to join as there was no number 13 — in winter flying suit worn over uniform.

On 9 May 1943, six WFTD pilots arrived at New Castle: Dorothy Young, Alexandria, Virginia; Marjorie Gray, Grantwood, New Jersey; Jane Straughn, Washington, D.C.; Magda Tache, Scarsdale, New York; Marion Mackey, New York City; and Eleanor Boysen, New York City.

The first three classes to graduate from WFTD became WAFS pilots. All

When this group of women pilots arrived at Gunner Field, Alabama, they were the first girl pilots seen there, and the first women to eat in the mess hall. L to r, standing: Barbara Towne, Helen Richards, B. J. Erickson; front; Teresa James and Betty Gillies.

Opposite: Teresa James was Flight Leader on a trip from Alberta, Canada, to Jackson, Tennessee, in 1943. From l to r: back row, Delphine Bohn (Amarillo, Texas), Nancy Batson (Birmingham, Alabama), Florene Miller (Odessa, Texas), and Teresa James; front row, Katherine Rawls Thompson (Olympic Swin Champion, Ft. Lauderdale, Florida) and Phyllis Burchfield (Titusville, Pennsylvania), in WAF uniforms. (Photo courtesy Scott Hubbard Features)

The WASP wings.

these women, plus the original 25, were part of the WAFS until 5 August 1943, when they were incorporated into the "WASP" — Women Airforce Service Pilots.

It appeared that the USAAF had finally decided to accept the women as separate but equal. Jackie Cochran was named director of women pilots and Nancy Love was appointed the WASP executive on the staff of the ATC's Ferrying Division.

WFTD graduates had worn wings that Cochran had made; the WAFS had worn the Civilian Air Transport Command pilot wings.

WASP Class 43-W-8, in December 1943, was the first to receive the officially issued regulation wings, bearing the official WASP insignia. These were redesigned, smaller wings, contrived from regulation pilot wings, with a satin-finish silver piece replacing the shield.

It was in 1944 that the WASP pilots received the uniforms provided by Cochran who outfitted them in blue slacks, battle jackets, and berets. The class of 44-W-1, graduating in February 1944, was the first to wear these Santiago blue uniforms.

Upon completion of the WASP training program, the graduating women had three choices. They could fly as instructors, as ferry pilots, or as test pilots. Five of Class 44-W-1 chose the latter. Margaret Weiss was one of these.

She recalls many instances when problems developed during the tests. Once at Williams Air Force Base near Phoenix, Arizona, she earned the respect of a male commander, who had been angry and profane at the idea of women on "his" field. But when he realized how well Weiss handled a particular emergency, he was eager to make up for his unreasonable attitude.

The mission of the pilots in the Ferrying Division was to move aircraft as needed to support the build-up of the Armed Forces. They delivered only within the continental limits of the U.S. and Canada and did not ferry to Britain. There was one time, however, in September 1943, when Nancy Love and Betty Gillies were assigned to take a B-17 four-engine bomber to England. Men had been griping about this assignment, so Colonel Tunner cleared the project with General Arnold's chief of staff while Arnold was in London. The women flew as far as Goose Bay, Labrador, without incident, where they had to wait for weather to clear before continuing. Just as they were about to depart on the last leg to England, they received a message from General Arnold saying they couldn't continue as he wanted women limited to domestic ferrying only. Later this was made into an Air Forces regulation.

The WASP ferried combat aircraft from factories to modification centers, to ports of embarkation, to combat training fields, to primary, basic, and advanced flying schools, to artillery bases, and to tow-target squadrons.

One of the towing squadrons was based at Eagle Pass Army Air Field, Texas. Starting in February 1943, WAFS pilots at the AAF Training Command's advanced pilot school at Eagle Pass had established themselves as queens of the upper air over that Rio Grande borderland area. By October 1943, the 17 pilots on duty at Eagle Pass — now WASPs — had amassed a total of approximately 9,000 hours of military flying time, just about enough to make two and one-half trips to the moon, flying at speeds of 150 mph. They logged this time by flying tow-target ships for gunnery students at this advanced flying school. The job of towing the oblong white-sleeve target was vital, demanding pilot endurance and stability. The WASP pilots performed that duty as capably as any group of men fliers.

The WASP established an excellent accident record at Eagle Pass. During one period, they flew a total of 3,000 hours with no accidents. The mishaps which did occur were minor, involving no fatalities. Margaret Holburn was the WASP Commanding Officer at Eagle Pass in 1943. Her previous assignment had been at South Plains Army Air Field, Lubbock, Texas, towing gliders with the twin-engine Lockheed Lodestar.

Other women based at Eagle Pass AAF were instrument-trained and qualified to fly the B-26 Martin Marauder medium bomber, used primarily for transition flight training. Powered by two Pratt & Whitney R-2800 Double Wasp 18-cylinder radial engines, each capable of 1,850 hp, this aircraft was nicknamed "Baltimore Flying Prostitute," or "Widow Maker," by the men

WAR DEPARTMENT
A. A. F. Form No. 99
Revised May 14, 1943

WAR DEPARTMENT
ARMY AIR FORCES
—
MEMORANDUM RECEIPT

*DEBIT   *CREDIT

No._____

Station_____ Date___23 August 1943____

Issuing organisation_____

*Issued by
*Turned in by }_____ Miss T. James _____

QUANTITY	UNIT	PART NO.	ARTICLE
1	ea		P-47 type aircraft, Serial No. 42-75032

I acknowledge receipt of the above-listed Air Corps property;

William W. Russell III
WILLIAM W. RUSSELL, 111,
1st Lt., AC,
Receiving Officer.

* Strike out words not applicable.   ☆ u. s. government printing office : 1943   16—9965-1   (Official designation)

AAF Memorandum Receipt.

who flew it because it was made in Baltimore and it had no visible means of support with its wing area seemingly too small for the weight of the plane. The early models of the B-26 had a bad track record and the male pilots avoided it whenever possible. Cochran asked General Arnold to let her asssign 25 WASP pilots to fly the B-26, and they did a fine job. Not having heard the rumors about the plane, they had no fear of it. It wasn't long before the male pilots declared the B-26 a safe airplane.

Teresa describes the problems with the B-26:

> . . . They were killing men like crazy. The men were trying to pull the airplane off too fast and it was losing lift. That was the Martin with the straight wing. You had to get it up to flying speed.

Neil McCray, an instructor from Erie, Pennsylvania, had told Teresa, "If you fly the B-26 — and I've flown it — keep that sucker on the runway until you see the end of it coming up, then let it fly itself off and you'll have no problem."

The WASP also helped the AAF Training Command overcome a problem the male pilots had with the B-29 Superfortress four-engine bomber. Colonel Paul W. Tibbets, pilot of the *Enola Gay,* of later A-bomb reknown, in charge of the training program, found two WASP pilots at Eglin Field — Dora

Fifinella, the logo of the WASPs. (Courtesy of Teresa James)

Dougherty and Dorothea Johnson. Both were veterans of Camp Davis and were currently towing targets for pursuit gunnery practice. Tibbets worked with Dougherty and Johnson for three days. He did not tell them of the engine fires that made the men fearful of flying the bomber. He just had them taxi out and take off as soon as the engines were running, without stopping for a conventional "runup." He then had a new B-29 on the field outfitted for demonstration flights with the WASP mascot, the winged pixie caricature *Fifinella,* and the name *Lady Bird* painted on the nose, and had the two women set out for the very-heavy-bomber base at Alamagordo, New Mexico. For several days, they flew back and forth across the state carrying pilots and crew members who would soon be sent to the Pacific. The ease with which they handled the plane put the men who had refused to fly it to shame. Word soon reached Washington, and Major General Barney B. Giles, Chief of Air Staff, sent an order that the WASP pilots must stop flying the big bomber immediately. But Tibbets' training tactic had worked. The men could no longer claim that the B-29 was dangerous to fly. Dougherty and Johnson only had a few weeks of flying what was then the largest bomber in the Air Forces, making them 2 of only about 100 pilots at the time who knew how to fly the Superfortress.

By 1944, Nancy Love reported that her "elite corps" had 123 pilots since the original WAFS had been formed in late 1942.

A total of 1,830 pilots had been selected to train for the WASPs, out of some 25,000 applicants or inquiries. They logged more than 60 million miles in the course of their training. But despite all their accomplishments, the program was short-lived. Early in 1944, militarization of the WASP was recommended by the Military Affairs Committee of the House of Representatives, but the bill failed to pass. And so, by December 1944, with the graduation of the final class from Sweetwater, Texas, the WASP was deactivated. The principal disadvantage of not militarizing the WASP was that the women were deactivated without any rights or veterans' benefits, with no reserve status, and with no insurance for survivors. These women worked parallel to men, doing the same job, taking the same risks, but they were not rewarded with equal pay or privileges.

Demobilization of the WASP on 20 December 1944 was costly to the war effort and the taxpayer. It deprived the Air Transport Command of approximately 200 expert ferrying pilots as well as tow-target pilots, test pilots, and administrative pilots, and others involved in the war effort. It cost a million dollars to train men to do their jobs, and it hampered the delivery of planes during the four to six months that these men were being trained. It also prevented the men who were being transferred to ferry duty from completing training for specialized combat tasks. Furthermore, the women pilots had 18 months experience which could not be replaced. Approximately 50 percent of

Fer Div Form No. 75-10E. 1 July 1944
RESTRICTED

AIRCRAFT DELIVERY MEMORANDUM

HEADQUARTERS, 552ND AAF BASE UNIT (2ND FERRYING GROUP) FERRYING DIVISION, ATC
NEW CASTLE ARMY AIR BASE, WILMINGTON 99, DELAWARE

TO **Teresa D. James, 2nd F.O. (WASP)**   Date **14 Aug 44** Memo No. **2704**
_____
    Pilot

_____   _____
    Co-Pilot   Engineer

_____   _____
    Navigator   Radio Operator
Deliver aircraft described below to destination indicated.
Additional Instructions: _____

Upon completion of delivery, crew will: _____ **ret to NCAAB, Wilm, Del.** ____

Signed *Harold E Shively* / S/2AC *Asst Domestic oper off*
    Name and Rank   Official Position

AIRCRAFT DELIVERY RECEIPT

1. Aircraft: **RA-25A** _____   **XXXXXXX 41-1842**
    Model   Serial No.

    C-56856
_____
    Account   Proj. No or Block Priority   Flight Order No.
CLASSIFIED EQUIPMENT INSTALLED ON AIRCRAFT:

_____

OTHER EQUIP. AS LISTED ON A.C. FORMS NO. 263A & 263B (Cross out 263B if not applicable)

2. Delivery:
    To: **CO, Aberdeen Proving Ground**
            Recipient Organization
    At: **Phillips Fld, Aberdeen, Md.**
            Delivery Point – – – – Date – – – – –
    From: **CO, Walterboro AAF**
            Releaser
    At: **Walterboro, S.C.**
            (Pick-up Point)

3. Receipt: I acknowledge receipt of aircraft with contents as noted above, and
Forms 263A and 263B (Cross out 263B if not applicable)

            Aberdeen Proving Ground
            Recipient Organization
Distribution:
Copy 1- Home Station of Pilot
Copy 2- Pilot   Signature of person authorized to sign
Copy 3- Aircraft Recipient   for Recipient Organization
Copy 4- Office issuing memorandum

            Rank and official position of signer
Must be signed IN INK or INDELIBLE PENCIL, LEGIBLY, by an AUTHORIZED Representative of the Recipient Organization. RESTRICTED

Aircraft Delivery Memorandum.

all pursuit ferrying in the United States had been done by WASP pilots.

Colonel William Bruce Arnold (USAF, Ret.), son of General Henry H. Arnold, worked to change the status of these women many years later. In 1977 he said,

```
A-25 1750 HP. Consumption 90 G.P.H.
3 Tanks- F-90/W-105 ea.  OIL- 25 gal.
 Cruise about 200.

BEFORE START
Form I
Seat & Rudder
Altimeter
Ignition Off
Controls Free
Fuel Selector- T/O Left Main
 Switch to Fuselage in Air
Landing Gear  Down
Flaps closed-neutral
Circuit Breakers -B-ON
Other Switches Off
Generator-Battery-ON
Prop-Circuit Breaker "ON"
 Auto-Inc R.P.M.
Cowl Flaps-Open
Supercharger-Low
Mixture to I.C.O.
Throttle Cracked
Carb Heat Direct or Ram-
Emerg Fuel Pump ON 7-8lbs
Starter to starter to mesh
Prime(Max 5 Sec)
Ignition Both
Mixture Full Rich.
Warm Up:
1000RPM till oil temp 55,
Fuel Pump Off.
_____

BEFORE TAKE*OFF

Ck. Gas Tanks
Ck. Flaps-Pressure on rt instrument
 should read 1000 LBS, Left 0
Bomb bays "closed"
Mixture full rich
Supercharger "LOW"
Cowl flaps closed
Wing flaps neutral.
Trim tabs AIL o --Elv. 1 --Rud-7
Check Prop 1200 Manual
then to Automatic
Mags at 2000 in manual
Prop to Auto.
CK. Ammeter
Emerg Fuel Pump "ON"
Harness Lock
Tailwheel lock
Landing Gear Lock
T.O.-40"-2800
Climb 35"-2300-140M.P.H.
Cruise 28"-2100
Fuel Pump"OFF" at 1000ft.
```

```
BEFORE LANDING

Fuel Best Tank
Supercharger- low
Mixture Full rich
Emerg Fuel Pump "ON"
Prop 2600 RPM.
Cowl Flaps Closed
Tail Wheel Locked
Gear Down - 200
Harness Locked
Flaps -under 150 - 30 to 45 o
Glide 120


AFTER LANDING

Cowl flaps Open
Prop-Full increase
Flaps up
Tailwheel unlocked
Run at 1000 RPM
Mixture to I.C.OI.
All Switches off
Rudder trim sets to aileron o reading


Fuel 6-7 (MAX 10)
Oil pressure 80-85 (MAX90)
 Oil Temp. 50-70 (MAX 85)
Head Temp.- ground (MAX 205)
          climb (MAX 248)
 R.P.M. (MAX 3100)
Climb-35/31- 2300-2100
Cruise 28"- 2000

HYDRAULIC EMERGENCY

Put gear in down position- Close NO.1
valve- Pump gear down- NO.1 valve shuts
off turrets, armament- "BUT" operates
brakes, flaps, gear.
If above fails-- leave NO.1 valve
 closed & open NO.3. Put gear in down
position & rock ship laterally. There
will be no flaps , brakes or tailwheel
```

A-25 Checklist.

Envy and jealousy of a group of male civilian pilots who feared the WASPs would replace them and thus force them into combat or the draft, manifested itself in a strong lobby that was able to kill the Army Air Forces-sponsored militarization bill of 1944. It is our intention now to secure for the present living WASP members the veterans' privileges which were denied them over thirty years ago.

A bill, which was finally passed in 1977, provided some assistance to the estimated 900 WASP pilots still living. It provided recognition to "the Women Air Force Service Pilots for their services to their country during World War II, by deeming such service to have been active duty in the Armed Forces of the United States for purposes of laws administered by the Veterans Administration."

Chapter 6

The Ferry Queen

The largest plane Teresa had flown prior to joining the WAFS had been the 225 hp Waco. Even so, when Lieutenant French checked her out in the 175 hp Fairchild PT-19, he said that her downwind turns weren't the way they should be as she executed 180 degree overhead landings.

Teresa remembers:

> I looked at him like he was crazy, and then reflected, perhaps I'm giving him a rough time because I was slipping the airplane in like I used to do at tiny fields with trees on one end, and high tension wires on the other, where you had to [do that] to get it down. That maddened French. He said, "That's not the Army way of flying."

The women were given 25 hours of flying time, dual and solo, with two objectives. The first was to be sure that their flying was not sloppy. The Air Forces required a degree of precision not usually demanded in even the best civilian flight schools.

> When they tell you to make a 90 degree turn, they don't want 89 or 91 degrees. "You've got to hit it on the nose, Sister, and I don't mean maybe!" was the instruction issued by the Army.

The second objective was learning how to execute Army traffic patterns in the interest of safety. These patterns are the rules of the roads in the air. The

WAFS already knew them, as the Civil Aeronautics Administration had prescribed them for civilians. But the Army was different, with its own individual procedure that had to be followed to a "T." This explains the harried hangar flying and tracing of diagrams in the airport dust.

Most of the training was done in the Taylorcraft L2-B, even though the women would ferry the Liaison Taylorcraft L4-B and the Primary Trainer Fairchild PT-19A. They had to be checked out on ground handling, takeoffs, level and climbing turns, gliding turns with power, straight and level flight, approaches and landings, stalls (power on and power off), straight and in turns, spins, chandelles, maximum climbing turns, steep banks, eights on pylons, forced landings, and 360 degree landings. If a WAFS pilot could pass a checkout on all these points and pass her written exam in ground school, the 25 hours of flight time were not a strict requirement.

Teresa's initial flight check had been on 21 September 1942 in the L2-B with Lieutenant Saccio. The following week, Lieutenant Tracy flew with her. His remarks in her log book included: "9-23-42, student needs more study of traffic pattern; 9-24, work shows improvement today." She flew with Lieutenant French on 26 September who wrote: "student judgment very sound, using some cross rudder, not holding true course in power-off work." Then Teresa flew a PT-19A on 1 October with Lieutnant Starbuck who said: "stalls OK, poor entry into traffic pattern. Progress and judgment fair." On 2 October Teresa flew with Lieutenant Tracy in the PT-19A for her final dual flight — her flight log read: "work planned in a satisfactory manner."

Her training in October included a cross-country and return on the 8th to Hagerstown, Maryland, where Fairchild had a plant. The next day she practiced takeoffs and landings at the DuPont Field, not far from New Castle AAB, in a Fairchild PT-19A. She completed the flight-training phase with a solo cross-country and return on 18 October in a PT-19A from New Castle to Scranton and Middletown, Pennsylvania.

Understanding military forms was especially important as the ferry pilot was responsible for all the paperwork connected with an airplane from the time he or she took over the ship at the factory until it was signed for by the proper officer at the base to which it was delivered.

Upon completion of the WAFS training course, New Castle AAB was Headquarters, but the women could expect to be assigned to any part of the country on individual ferry jobs. Each ferry group had both a Flight and a Sub-Flight Leader, but those designations applied only when in the air. The Flight Leader was responsible for navigation. On the ground, when the job was completed, there were no more regulations away from stations than there would be for any other civilians.

After Teresa had checked out in the PT-19A, there was very little additional time for flight training, though she got six hours in the BT-13 seven months

A pilot briefing for the first PT-19 trip for Fairchild Aviation from the factory at Hagerstown, Maryland. L to r: Betty Gillies, Nancy Batson, Esther Nelson, H. M. Clark, Teresa James, Ev Sharp, and Captain Franks, Operations Officer.

later. She recalls, "They wanted to make sure that we didn't crack up those little grasshoppers." Then she got six hours dual in an AT-6 and about eight hours dual in a twin-engine AT-9. That was the extent of training prior "to checking myself out in pursuit airplanes. I checked myself out in the P-47 and P-51."

Early in October, Teresa sat up for two nights on the train to spend one day at home. She enjoyed the time with her family, but wasn't sure it was worth the agony that followed. Her cab pulled up in front of BOQ14 at 7:55 the following Monday morning.

> I had already worked myself into a nervous state of collapse, afraid I would be late to Roll Call at 8:00. Records were broken in taking off and putting on clothing . . . to say nothing of the five-block sprint in as many seconds, flat! . . . I was dead. Then came the order to report to the hospital for an Army 64 physical. Of all days. . . .
>
> My first thought was to go on over and pack. There wasn't a chance for me to pass it in my fatigued condition. I had visions of the stethoscope and other medical gadgets registering all my weaknesses. Besides, they would probably spin me around in a chair a hundred or so revolutions. My heart was pounding; hearts have to be sound. My eyelids wouldn't stay open; eyes must be perfect! Those unforgettable five hours make up an experience I do not wish to repeat. All I can say is that I must be disgustingly healthy.

The 6th of October 1942 had been a Red Letter Day. Teresa was sworn into the WAFS, and Betty Gillies was made official Director of Women Pilots. Just a few days before, the first planes had left for England. Many years later, on 22 July 1985, at the dedication of the WAFS Plaque at the Greater Wilmington Airport (formerly New Castle AAB and renamed New Castle County Airport in 1990), Betty Gillies recalled those days of 1942:

> We had been at NCAAB less than two weeks when Colonel Robert Baker invited the still small contingent of WAFS to stand with him during Review of the base. It was in the very early hours of Saturday morning, 3 October 1942. As we were all standing at attention in front of about 30 A-30s, a B-24, piloted by Bruce Gimbel, took off with six P-38s right behind and headed for England . . . the first flight of P-38s to attempt a trans-Atlantic crossing! As the 38s formed on the B-24, our NCAAB Band struck up the Air Forces song: "Off We Go into the Wild Blue Yonder"! It

was a thrilling sight and a very moving one. How very fortunate we were to be able to play a small part in this!

Colonel Henry R. Johnston (USAF, Ret.) also was on the speakers' rostrum that day in 1985, as President of the Wilmington Warriors, a group made up of the ferry pilots during World War II. When Betty Gillies finished speaking, Colonel Johnston surprised her by stepping forward and saying that he was one of the P-38 pilots on that first ferry flight.

Teresa James described her thoughts at that time in her diary, after watching the P-38s leave for Europe.

> There's something a little different to describe about soloing a plane with a big star on it. We were standing watching the men in review this morning. They were just passing the stand when another B-24 and six P-38s took off for foreign territory and flew right over them. A goose pimple moment!

An Operations Order for the WAFS was issued on 7 October 1942 under the letterhead of the 2nd Ferrying Group Headquarters, Ferry Division, ATC, NCAAB, Wilmington, Delaware, although the women had not yet finished their training.

> Ops Order 269:
> Under the authority of the Secretary of War, dated December 24, 1941, the following named Civilian pilots are hereby directed to proceed from NCAAB, Wilmington, Delaware to the Fairchild Aircraft Factory, Hagerstown, Maryland and return in airplane type and serial number as indicated opposite their names below as required under W.A.F.S. Transition School:
>
> Betty H. Gillies: Leader — L-2B (43-68)
> Helen Mary Clark: Sub-Leader — L-2B (43-69)
> Teresa D. James: L-2B (43-70)
>
> By order of Colonel Baker. Signed by Onas P. Matz, Captain, Air Corps, Operations Officer.

Each group of planes would have a Flight Leader who appointed a woman to navigate each leg. The Flight Leader flew in back. If the lead woman got lost, the Flight Leader would take over.

After Teresa and seven other women finished the course with their cross-country training in PT-19s, Teresa didn't find the new green-gray uniforms very attractive:

> They were designed for utility and not glamour, which reminds
> me I certainly hated the snip, snip of the scissors that cut my long
> hair, but this is really no place for it. Faces are going to be lucky if
> they get any attention.

The next night Teresa slept well and dreamed that she was ferrying a
bomber:

> Well, they didn't say we could, but they didn't say we couldn't,
> either.

By 22 October, orders for the first actual delivery came through. Six of the
eight new "graduates" were called in. They knew nothing, except that they
were going. They had no wings, no insignia yet, just plain uniforms and
impatience to be flying.

From the outset, the WAFS weren't allowed to have cameras or take
pictures. If asked what they were doing, they couldn't tell anyone that they
were flying airplanes. Their work was to be secret; in fact, it was one of the
best kept "war secrets" until LOOK magazine published an article on 6
February 1943 titled "The WAFS — A Squadron of 25 Girls is Leading the
Way for U.S. Women Fliers," with five pages of photographs. After that,
interest of the press was intense. The women were no longer anonymous,
ordinary ferry pilots.

They packed their B-4 bags for this first delivery. Teresa said,

> There is no medium of measure whereby their total capacity can
> be stated. No matter how much is put in them, there is still room for
> one colt and a medium-sized cook stove. I took four or five things I
> didn't need and left several I did, but that was not the fault of the
> equipment. After all, foresightedness was not one of the items
> issued at the Sub-Depot.

This ferrying job was to take planes from the Piper factory at Lock Haven,
Pennsylvania, to Mitchel Field on Long Island. Teresa recalled,

> One of the officers flew us out to Lock Haven to pick up our
> planes in an old Boeing [247] that was about ready to fall apart.
> Gillies was co-pilot. We looked at the scenery with all the avidness
> of passengers on their first flight and got a big kick, as well as a
> bump, out of the rotten landing our pilot made. He admitted it was a

```
                    HEADQUARTERS
                    2ND FERRYING GROUP
          FERRYING DIVISION - AIR TRANSPORT COMMAND
                  NEW CASTLE ARMY AIR BASE
                  WILMINGTON, DELAWARE




                        CERTIFICATE




      This is to certify that on the ___12th___ day of ___November___ ,

1942, _____Teresa James_____ , successfully completed the

course of ground instruction prescribed for the Women's Auxiliary Ferrying

Squadron, 2nd Ferrying Group, Ferrying Division, Air Transport Command.
```

Robert H Baker

ROBERT H. BAKER
Colonel, Air-Corps
Commanding

OFFICIAL:

Richard Jordan

RICHARD H. JORDAN,
1st. Lieut., A.C.,
Officer In Charge of Ground Schools

Teresa James' Certificate of completion of general instruction for the Women's Auxiliary Ferrying Squadron, 12 November 1942.

"stinker." This was the first in a long series of appearances where necks were stretched to their full length and eyes literally popped out of faces. THE WAFS ARE COMING! THEY'RE GIRLS! LOOK! They would not have stared one-half as much had we been freaks from the circus side-show.

Little time was lost as there was a 25-mile an hour tail wind. We took off, amid speculative mutterings and mumblings, all flying

Cubs. Those little four-cylinder go-carts actually leaped into the air. Clarke had never flown such a light ship and we laughed when she said, "Jeepers! I just couldn't keep the thing on the ground."

The night was spent in Allentown, Pennsylvania, and it might well be called the Night of Horrors. We had been thoroughly trained and familiarized with the necessary forms. But that's like making an "A" in geometry at school and trying to apply the knowledge when you need to build a fence later in life.

Our second set-back came when we got a glimpse of ourselves in a full length mirror for the first time since donning our uniforms. Dead silence followed, then a profusion of why-didn't-you-tell-me? Something definitely had to be done, we voted, but there was nothing we could do, so we went to bed.

At sunrise they continued the flight. Gillies, being familiar with New Jersey and New York, took over navigation and they started for Mitchel Field. There were a number of bomb ranges along this route. Teresa said,

> We were told later that we had just flown over one between shots, but this fact was never confirmed. We learned, among other things, on this initial trip, not to believe everything we heard.

The WAFS were expected at the airport, and all personnel who could leave their posts waited in a group to watch them land. Teresa said,

> I can imagine the remarks that flew right and left. "Those dames! Why don't they get smart and let men run this Army?" "Steady men, we'll probably see some high bouncing and modernized ground loops!" "Line up fellows, and protect the buildings."

The six little Cubs approached the field and made six perfect landings. Gillies called home, and her family seemed very surprised to hear from her. Teresa noted:

> This was our first knowledge of the fact that families and friends of the WAFS expected us to fall off the face of the earth and never be heard from again.

There was time to kill before catching the train back to Wilmington, so Teresa and Del Scharr decided to see New York City while the other women dashed here and there. On the way to Radio City and the Rainbow Room, they marched right down Broadway in their strange-fitting trousers.

On sofa at Huntington Ho-
tel, Long Island, New York.
From l to r: Liz Pearce,
Helen Richey, and Teresa
James.

"The Slop Joint," a restaurant in Huntington, Long Island, near the Republic Factory. Front l to r, back row: Helen Richey, Liz Lundy, Jo Pitz, and Cecilia Hunter (who went to Alaska after the war and started a flying service); front row, Ruth Adams, Teresa James, Virginia Clair "Tex" Martin (who toted her .45 everywhere and wore cowboy boots), and Gert Messerve.

Shopping in Huntington, Long Island, Ruth Adams (now Dr.; once when doing a combat takeoff in a P-47, Adams wacked off a tree top with the gear, but there was no damage to the aircraft): l to r, Teresa James, Gertrude Merserve, and Liz Lundy.

Passersby took us for everything from Red Cross Volunteers to Junior Commandos. We hereby stake our claim to being the first WAFS in New York City.

Nobody missed the train to Wilmington. Clark brought her family to meet us. Her boys are ten and twelve years of age, and certainly something to be proud of. And, are they proud of their mother!

Back on the base, Captain Matz had been hospitalized for surgery. His first words on coming out of the anesthesia were, "Did the girls come through all right?"

When the ferry group arrived back at New Castle AAB, the women went directly to the Ready Room to wait for the next assignment. Those who were elsewhere on the base kept their ears open, waiting for their names to be read over the loudspeaker.

Another ferrying job took the WAFS pilots in L-4s from Lock Haven, Pennsylvania, to New Orleans, Louisiana. The last three to leave went on to

McComb, Mississippi, where they refueled. Teresa remembers the fellow with a keen sense of humor who sarcastically said, "I know exactly why you brought those in here for gas. You used exactly four drops."

The three women continued on to New Orleans. Teresa said,

> I will never forget that 40 miles of swamp country. Looking south and seeing nothing but marshy, bottomless-looking bogs where alligators thrive — what a place for a forced landing if the little "puddle jumper" had quit.

There were three airports in New Orleans — Municipal, Navy, and Army. Teresa added:

> Wonder of wonders, we found the right one. A fellow came in ahead of us, and broke his wing and prop. We thought "atta boy, fella, you crack 'em up, and we will bring you some more!"
>
> We had good weather as we flew south. It was clear and there was no wind. The planes practically flew themselves, but our legs got tired because of the limited amount of room, so we just propped them over the seat.
>
> We got in early, but that didn't help us any. The Lieutenant would not sign for the planes until they were inspected, so we waited patiently. After about an hour we discovered that particular officer had gone out to dinner instead of inspecting our planes. So we proceeded to go right after him with fire in our eyes! He finally signed the receipt, but with the notation that the planes were still to be checked.
>
> Jung Hotel was our destination, and it was crowded. We soon found out why. It was Saturday and Tulane was playing football. We wasted no time getting ready for dinner at Antoine's. It was really something — everything it was famous for was there. After dinner we saw more of New Orleans. It was a very nice experience.

Getting back to base after the delivery was not easy. The women were at the mercy of public transportation. They carried with them the TR (Transportation Request), which allowed them travel on any sort of commercial transportation without having to pay for it. However, as they were not allowed to return on military aircraft and many of the fields they delivered to were hundreds of miles from the commercial airports, they had to travel on trains or, even worse, buses jammed with wartime travelers. Sometimes they had to stand up for 200 miles to get to a commercial airfield.

Teresa's most memorable trip in November 1942 was ferrying an L-4B. At

5:00 p.m. on 9 November, Teresa, Betty Gillies, Cornelia Fort, Barbara Poole, Barbara Erickson, Barbara Towne, and Helen Richards boarded a train for Philadelphia where they had dinner and saw the movie *Wake Island*. Catching the 1:08 a.m. train to Lock Haven, Pennsylvania, they slept in Pullman berths. Accompanied by three young men, Lieutenants Triest, Jones, and Bally, they all had a merry time.

The women arrived at Lock Haven on 10 November at 6:40 in the morning, looking rather bedraggled. They spent the day sitting around the Fallon Hotel, waiting for the weather to clear, but it didn't — it was a typical rainy spell.

By 11 November, the weather was VFR, meaning visibility of three miles or more and a cloud ceiling of at least 1,000 feet. The flight of nine departed Lock Haven at 11:45 a.m., then stopped at Olmstead AB, Middletown, Pennsylvania, and at Quantico, Virginia, for gas. They flew in formation to Quantico where Lieutenant Triest left the group. The remaining eight continued on to Charlottesville, Virginia, where the mud was deep in places on the landing strip. Teresa recalled:

> It must have been raining for days. Everything was soggy and we tried to land on what looked like strips of grass, but Cornelia and Barb Poole nosed over when they set down. Their ships sustained busted props but no other damage. Fortunately, the rest of us hit a dry spot. All of those places were newly built and didn't have any runways. There was no pierced steel planking (PSP) in those days, so we landed in the mud, weeds, or whatever, and then had to dodge equipment on the way in. We went into places without control towers — you had to find your way in with a green light or whatever. It was especially primitive in the early part of the war.

During the fuel stop at Quantico, the Marines proudly assigned them a "Ladies Room," without a request. At many bases the personnel weren't as thoughtful, but the Marines provided true Virginia hospitality. On another occasion, when the WAFS had to stay overnight, a part of the Visiting Officers Quarters (VOC) was partitioned off with a sort of "wall of Jericho" and a sign posted, "Keep Out! Ladies Present."

Teresa's flight log entries for that trip included stops on 12 November at Danville, Virginia; Charlotte, North Carolina; and Spartanburg, South Carolina. On 13 November, she stopped at Toccoa and Atlanta, Georgia, and then at Opelika and Montgomery, Alabama. On the 14th, she departed Montgomery for Selma, Meridian, and finally Jackson, Mississippi. The pilot had to be capable of solving any problems of cross-country navigation as her mission proceeded. When clouds rendered visibility impossible, she had to navigate by "dead reckoning," computing a compass course from her maps.

Teresa also remembers the time she had to land a Piper Cub on the parade ground at West Point Military Academy. She used the flag as a windsock. There were no other aircraft there and a surprised commanding officer said, "What am I going to do with this aircraft?"

Teresa answered, "Please, just sign this memorandum receipt." She remembers, "The CO was more astounded than I was."

By 18 November the women were back in Lock Haven to repeat the trip with another batch of L-4Bs. This time they departed at 2:00 p.m., stopped in Middletown for gas, and remained overnight (RON'd) at Quantico. As before, the Marines had the situation under control in nothing flat. Major Harold Brown took the women in tow. They were put up very comfortably at the Officers Quarters, taken out for a drink and dinner, and then to the Officers Club. It was a very happy gathering.

One of the women, Cornelia Fort, was later killed in a bomber crash in Texas in 1943. She was the first woman in American history to die while on war duty. Because Cornelia was Nashville's first woman flight instructor, the state of Tennessee erected a historical marker at the airport which they had named after her. Shortly before her death, Cornelia wrote of her feelings, echoing the way most WASP pilots described the emotional impact of their service.

> They chatter about the glamour of flying. Well, any pilot can tell you how "glamorous" it is. We get up in the cold dark in order to get to the airport by daylight. We wear cumbersome flying clothes and a 30 pound parachute. You are either hot or cold; your lipstick wears off, and your hair gets straighter and straighter. You look forward all afternoon to a bath and a steak, and get the bath but rarely the steak. Sometimes you're too tired to even eat. None of us can put into words why we fly. . . . But I know it is dignity, self-sufficiency and pride of skill. I know it is the satisfaction of usefulness.

In addition to the tiring schedule, changes in temperature made trips and comfort difficult. Teresa said,

> When you left Hagerstown, Maryland, in the winter with an open cockpit PT-19, you had to have your winter gear on, the heavy pants, boots, and jacket. And, if you were going out West, as you moved into warmer weather, you shed clothes. Those open cockpits in winter were freezing. We had one trip I'll never forget.
>
> They sent us by train to Calgary, Alberta, Canada, to pick up PT-17s (Boeing Stearman). They couldn't use them up there [in

Teresa James' first flight as a Flight Leader, Great Falls, Montana, to Jackson, Tennessee. In back, l to r: Delphine Bohn, Nancy Batson, Florene Miller, Teresa James-Leader, Katherine Rawls, and Phyllis Burchfield.

winter] because of the cold weather — they were open cockpit trainers. That was my first flight as a Flight Leader. I had five gals — Katherine Thompson, Phyllis Burchfield, Delphine Bohn, Florene Miller, and Nancy Batson — with me. We departed Calgary on 12 December 1942. I was flying PT-17 serial number 42-15819 with a 220 hp Continental engine. When we got to Great Falls, Montana, it was 0 and it soon went down to -30. We had to wait until it warmed up to start those engines — we had to heat the oil.

They made chamois face masks for us with holes cut for the eyes and nose and mouth. You should have seen the girls — they looked like savages when they took off the masks, with their lipstick smeared around. Before we got to our destination, Jackson, Tennessee, we stopped at Billings, Montana; Casper, Wyoming; Denver, Colorado; Las Vegas and Albuquerque, New Mexico; Amarillo, Wichita Falls, and Dallas, Texas; Shreveport, Louisiana; Little Rock, Arkansas; and Memphis, Tennessee. Anyhow, luckily

Teresa James, Flight Leader for the first group to visit Great Falls, Montana, shown in her hotel room writing a RON telegram (note nail polish).

we got to Jackson. En route we had to go into small strips, and perhaps only one little area would be shoveled out. The guys used to tell us that the PT-17 is a real ground-looping son-of-a-gun, and I prayed that each girl got down, because we knew they were watching us from Washington.

Well, we made it, but boy was it cold. It was brutal. No one knew of the adversities of flying back in those days. The clothing wasn't insulated — just heavy, with over 40 pounds of gear . . . in our chute bags. Can you imagine navigating in an open cockpit through the chamois face mask? Even though we had goggles over our eyes, our nose and mouth were still exposed to the bitter cold.

Once again, the Army didn't care if it was -50; they just said "move it," and naturally, we were eager to fly.

That winter, the women ferried liaison-type planes and various trainers to bases scattered throughout the South and Midwest, and many up "Icicle Lane" to Canada. That was the most difficult ferrying of all, because the planes had no heat and no radios. It was cold, the winds were strong, and the ground was covered with snow and ice, which made it hard to identify landmarks for navigation.

Between trips, there was occassionally the chance to spend an evening in downtown Wilmington at the DuPont Hotel. It was not uncommon to see two women dancing together — jitterbug or polka — while the boyfriends and husbands "talked shop." Teresa was married to a pilot and her sister, Betty, was engaged to one — both of whom Teresa had taught to fly. Teresa remembers,

> Betty and I would polka or cha-cha until the band played a slow number. Our guys could waltz, so that was when they took over for some cheek-to-cheek dancing. On trips we stayed clear of the guys. They sounded like a broken record: "I might not come back." They would try to impress us by talking about the power and might of the aircraft they could fly. Anything to get you into the sack.

Teresa was the first WAFS pilot to fly a military plane coast-to-coast across the United States when she took a PT-19 from the Fairchild factory in Hagerstown, Maryland, to Paul Mantz in Burbank, California. On 17 February 1943, she departed Hagerstown for Lynchburg, Virginia, and on to Charlotte, North Carolina, and Athens, Georgia, taking the southern route because it was a lower altitude route and avoided the high mountain ranges. Five days and 14 new air bases later, she arrived in California.

West Coast factories and runways were disguised with trees planted on rooftops and nets with camouflage over everything else. All of California looked like countryside. Teresa remembers California:

> I'll never forget when I took that plane out to Burbank. The base was camouflaged for wartime.
>
> It was very hard to find Burbank Field. When I did, the camouflage threw off my depth perception which was essential to a safe landing. At each base the guys lined up, staring curiously, some asking questions, and most saying, "Gee, can you believe — it's a girl flying an Army airplane!"
>
> I felt like a celebrity.
>
> Flying in those days, you had no radio contact. You had to fly by the watch, the map, and your ground speed. At first we didn't use the radio ranges or beacons, which criss-crossed the country. We

Teresa James in winter uniform before leaving Hagerstown, Maryland, on coast-to-coast trip with a PT-19 for famed aviator Paul Mantz in Burbank, California.

just marked a course on our maps every ten miles. You moved your finger along the map, and away you went.

The women had to be careful not to drop a map in a plane like the BT-13, because the way the plane was designed, it was impossible to reach down to the floor. In fact, it really was not the floor; the map slid all the way to the bottom of the aircraft.

I'll tell you, that was a long trip from Maryland to California over country I'd never seen, and I didn't know what I was getting into. Back in those days you took your chances. When you left, you called ahead to see what the weather was. It might be clear at the destination, but there was no way of knowing what the weather was doing in between. It was wild; I ran into weather like you wouldn't believe. We would get down on the deck, or do a 180 and get back.

Weathered in at Pensacola, Florida, the women found time for a party with Navy pilots. From l to r, Teresa James, Jill McCormick, and Irene Gregory.

Teresa James on the right with Ginny Simms of the "Call for Philip Morris" program, after doing a skit on the program in Burbank, California.

The strips were hard to identify — they were just little grass things. So we went through two years of hazardous cross-country. By the grace of God, we got there. My worst trip was the first one to California. I had never flown over mountain passes. It never occured to me that it was hazardous.

After all the furor she had created flying cross-country, Teresa was thrilled to meet the great Paul Mantz in California:

I had watched him fly in the 1930s at the National Air Races in Cleveland. He told me he would take me on a tour of the studios, never dreaming what was in store for me. I stayed in the Beverly Hills Hotel and, of course, the uniform with wings caused a sensation.

Life had certainly become exciting for the WAFS pilot. After a good night's sleep, Teresa had breakfast with movie stars Walter Houston and Ted Lewis. Spencer Tracy came over to their table to speak to Houston. After breakfast,

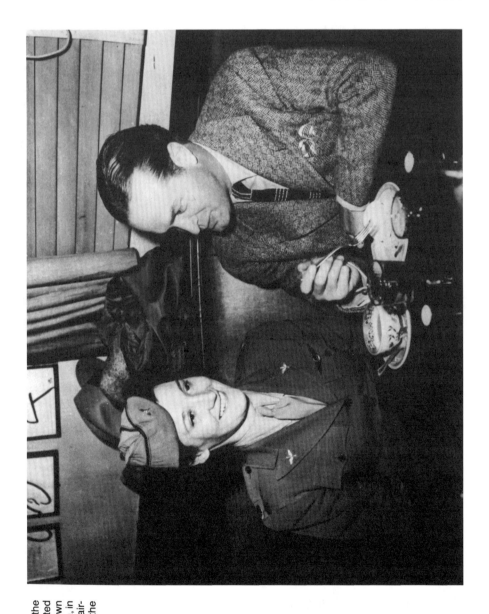

The first Flight Leader for the WAFS, Teresa James chatted with Bob Hope in The Brown Derby, Hollywood, California, in 1943 after delivering an airplane for a movie about the WAFS.

Teresa James with Marine Boxing champion Barney Ross at the Beverly Hills (California) Hotel, 1943.

the manager of the Beverly Hills Hotel arranged for Teresa to be taken to the 20th Century-Fox Studio where she was met by Mr. Fox himself, who took her to the set of *Stormy Weather.* Cab Calloway, Bojangles Robinson, and Irving Mills spent the afternoon with her and were all interested in hearing about her flying career.

That evening, Frank Long, swimming instructor of the stars, Jackie Cooper, and Teresa went to the Palladium. Benny Goodman, who was playing there, took Teresa up on stage and introduced her to the huge crowd. Later they all wound up at Romano's where Teresa met Louella Parsons and Marlene Dietrich.

The next day Teresa had breakfast with Father Flannagan of Boy's Town and met Baron Rothschild.

During her later cross-country missions, Teresa met many other movie stars and was asked to appear in a short Warner Brothers film about the women in the air war. She recalls a pleasant evening spent at the home of Bob Hope and his wife, and she made a special appearance on the Ginny Simms radio show. She also met sport figures like Barney Ross, the fighter, who was then in uniform.

Chapter 7

Heavy Iron

July 20, 1943

NEW CASTLE ARMY AIR BASE

Wilmington, Delaware

Miss Teresa James
WAF Squadron
New Castle Army Air Base
Wilmington, Delaware

Dear Miss James:

Perhaps this letter will amuse you or cause some other reaction. However, I shall send it to you anyway.

I am one of the Control Tower operators at this base coming here 6 weeks ago from a fighter base in Mass.

At this base the entire complement of planes consisted of P-47s.

In the course of my 3 months work there I saw many landings and takeoffs of the P-47. However, in all fairness, I must pass along the word to you that your landings both on your check-out flight about two weeks ago and again today's are easily classed among the best I have witnessed. There wasn't any sign of bouncing or

Left and opposite page:
Teresa James in the P-47.

swaying as you landed and your spacing on the runway for initial
point of contact was also good. It's too bad that you couldn't show
some of our fighter pilots how to land a P-47.

This probably amuses you, but good work should be recognized
by some slight token. A P-47 is a "lot" of airplane for anyone to
handle and you did swell.

Would be glad to hear your reaction to this letter. Its the first of
its kind I have ever written — any comment appreciated.

Yours,

C. I. Walker

P.S.   Might I have the pleasure of meeting you some evening next
week? Would appreciate the privilege very much.

C. I. Walker

Cpl. Chas. I. Walker
Det. 22d Fwys Com Sq c/o 344th Air Base Sqdn.
NCAAB
Wilmington, Delaware.

The P-47 was the heaviest fighter the WAFS flew. It weighed 12,500
pounds, had a 2,400 hp engine, and was twice the size of the British Spitfire. It
was a big step up after flying light aircraft. The cockpit had only enough room
for a single pilot, so a first flight had to be solo. Pursuit-type flying had been
practiced in the AT-6, but even so, that aircraft had a much smaller, 450 hp
engine. Pursuit-type landings were simulated by diving the AT-6 at the runway
at 120 mph and then pulling back on the stick at the precise moment when the
tires were about to touch.

Teresa's mother came to visit the week of Teresa's checkout and was in the
Chapel, saying the Rosary for her daughter the day of the flight. Teresa recalls:

> They never should have told me till about five minutes ahead of
> time, but as it happened, I had all night to worry about it. There
> were . . . a lot of people sitting out in that Control Tower . . . .
> Betty Gillies was the first girl to check out in the P-47, but I guess
> the brass just happened to be at the base.

Teresa was checked out by Captain Charles Bing, who stood on the wing while she sat on her seat-pack parachute in the single-seat cockpit. He made her go through all the emergency procedures. She remembers him saying, "When you take off, you're going to be 20 miles out past New Castle before you get the gear up. . . ."

Teresa thought of what one of her early flying instructors, Edgar P. "Pete" Goff, had taught her — to take an unfamiliar aircraft upstairs where you had plenty of altitude for safety and simulate landings until you got to know the aircraft's characteristics and landing speed. Not only was Goff a great instructor, but he was the first to make up a condensed map of the airways, like today's Jeppesen's or NOS (National Oceanic Survey) charts. A salesman for Stinson planes, an airline pilot, a corporate pilot, and a CAA Aeronautics Inspector, Goff flew for the military and later with the Link Company. He went to Vietnam as liaison officer for Decca Navigation Systems Inc., where he helped set up navigation aids for air traffic in 1963.

Teresa remembers clearly:

> What Bing said prior to my takeoff was "go up and practice some stalls and spins." I just looked at him. I knew he was being facetious.
>
> So, as I taxied out, I went over and over the emergency procedures. When I got to the end of the duty runway, I sat there maybe five extra minutes before I got up enough guts to call the Tower with "ready for takeoff." I started rolling down the runway. I had never flown an aircraft with that much horsepower. It pushed me back against the seat, and I was just rolling along gently — I didn't ram the throttle in fast. I noticed the speed increase as I went down the runway. I had that thing off before I passed midfield and got the gear up quickly and trimmed it out.
>
> That thing was a pussycat. But I had heard so many tales about how hard it was to fly, when it actually was an easy airplane to handle. I took it up to altitude, did some tight turns, and approach stalls. Then I brought it in and landed it, and it sat down nicely. I thought, "Wow — I'm down!"
>
> So, I found out the mystique was just a lot of male stories. The next day, after my P-47 checkout, I went to Lock Haven to pick up a Cub. Now, that did something to your ego. I flew a P-47 again about a month later. There were a couple of PT-19 trips to Oklahoma and one out West before I got in another P-47. We hopped from one type of aircraft to another — a Cub one day, then a P-47, then a PT-19, and on to a twin. You never knew what you were going to fly.

Teresa's first P-47 ferry flight, as per Operations Order 218, 6 August 1943,

Gertrude Tubbs congratulates Teresa James: "We always had bets on who could land shorter," said James.

directed her, under Flight Order C-10577, to report to the Factory Control Officer at the Republic Aviation Corporation at Farmingdale, Long Island, New York, and to deliver the aircraft to the Commanding Officer, 338th Fighter Group, Dale Mabry Field, Tallahassee, Florida, to obtain the usual receipts, and then to return without delay to NCAAB, Wilmington, Delaware. This she did.

Another trip Teresa remembers vividly was a PT-19 flight from Hagerstown to Oklahoma.

> . . . The first leg of our flight took us to Pittsburgh, my home town. It was nearly dusk when we landed. I wanted to tie the ships down outside of Base Operations but the Lieutenant said, "Nope, we gotta hangar them." Despite my objections, we had to taxi down a cobblestone ramp to the hangar.
>
> Bad weather moved in and for two days I celebrated St. Pat's day with my family. We prepared to depart Allegheny County Airport on a bright, sunny, cold day. Taxiing up the cobblestone ramp we had to use a lot of power, and I was a wreck worrying about the

Gertrude Meserve Tubbs at Republic Aviation, New York, picking up a P-47D in 1944.

A Recon car at Farmingdale, Long Island, going from the Operations Office to the hotel. Teresa James is in the back, with Ruth Adams, Gertrude Tubbs, and Jo Pitz; Sergeant Rosenbloom is in front.

"We had to pay full price to go to the movies" in Farmingdale, New York, near the Republic factory. From front of line: Jo Pitz, Gertrude Meserve, Teresa James, Ruth Adams, Cecilia Hunter, "Tex" Martin, Liz Lundy, and Helen Richey.

prop propelling stones through the fabric wings or nicking the blades.

When we landed at Columbus for gas, we did discover deep nicks in Nelson's and Bernheim's props. I worried that they would set up a vibration that might cause a propeller to come off in flight, but decided to fly on to Indianapolis where we tried to get new props. None were available; we stayed in town that night.

We got to the airport early the next morning only to be told that a Captain taxiing a C-47 hit the leading edge of Bernheim's ship with his rudder. We were delayed until early afternoon while the damage was repaired.

The flight took off for Belleville, Illinois, a little southeast of St. Louis, landing at Scott Field. The props were checked while a truck gassed the planes. Bernheim and Nelson said that so far there hadn't been any vibration.

Teresa proceeded to the weather office and went up to the counter to have the clearance signed for the next leg to Springfield, Missouri. The Captain

At the Republic Aviation factory, Farmingdale, Long Island, New York: seated, Anna Flynn, Ginny Alleman, Rita Monahan, _____; standing, Teresa James, Liz Lundy, Gertrude Meserve, and Pat Lawler.

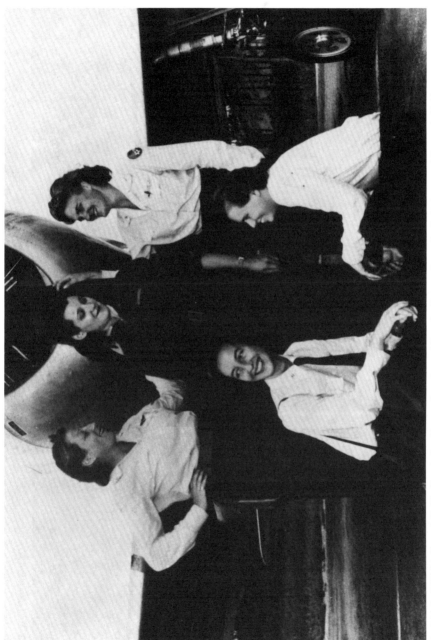

A 1944 P-47 flight. From left: Sis Bernheim, Teresa James, and Cecelia Hunter; front: Emily Heister and Gertrude Tubbs.

Gertrude S. Tubbs in a P-47D.

barked out, "Who is your Flight Leader?"

Teresa replied smiling, "I am, Sir."

The Captain proceeded to berate her for cutting out a B-17 that was coming in for a landing, and for ignoring a red light. Teresa said, "The Tower gave me a green light," but the Captain insisted that the light had been red. Teresa called the other women over to the counter and asked each one of them if they had got a green light to land, and they replied, "Yes."

The Captain's insistence that the women were in the wrong was irritating. Teresa told him,

> You know, we don't have radios, and if we inconvenienced the guy in the B-17, I suggest he talk to the Tower operator.

The women were getting the planes delivered in record time, a fact that the men seemed to resent. Teresa recalls,

> Before we arrived at NCAAB, the service pilots, including the flying sergeants, would take a couple of weeks to deliver an airplane. They would detour and see their girlfriends, or goof off. Along came the WAFS, and we were delivering like crazy. We got to destination and back in nothing flat. That caused resentment right there.

One of Teresa's most unforgettable flights started out innocently enough. She was assigned to deliver a P-47 from Farmingdale, New York, to Republic's modification center in Evansville, Indiana. It was mid-summer and Betty Gillies said, "You don't need anything, you're coming right back," so when Teresa left she just had on her tan shirt and gray slacks.

After battling a severe rainstorm and a perspiration-saturated, dirty flight suit, Teresa delivered the P-47 to Evansville. Before she could dry out, or even comb her wet, tangled hair, she was given a flight assignment to take a P-47 to Long Beach, California. Teresa said, "I don't have any clothes with me . . . but OK."

On this trip, the weather closed in and Teresa was stuck in Evansville for four days. When it cleared, the airplane wasn't ready. By that time a week had gone by and Teresa felt that now she smelled "like a damn nanny goat, wearing the same pants — it looked like I had basketballs, or cantaloupes, where the knees had got out of shape."

She finally left Evansville and delivered the P-47 to Long Beach.

> It was a scary trip. You used to watch the map and use your eyes to navigate, looking for ground reference points. How in hell we

Teresa James and Betty Gillies at the Evansville, Indiana, modification center with a P-47 James ferried in from Long Island. Gillies was the first woman to check out in the P-47.

ever got P-51s and P-47s across country without smashing anything, I'll never know. I never thought about it at the time. There wasn't much air traffic back then. I would pick out four check points ahead of me. I must have zig-zagged a lot in the air. I would drop one and add one. I was always alert and I never goofed off. I had tremendous trust. . . .

After the Operations Officer signed the P-47 off, he asked Teresa if she had ever flown a P-51? "Nope," she said. He told her to get the tech orders and read them.

By that time, it was 6:00 p.m. Teresa had heard how the fog rolls in at Long Beach, so she decided to call it a day and left to study the tech orders for the P-51.

The next morning, she went to Operations and took a first look at the aircraft. Inspecting its in-line engine, she thought it was nothing like the P-47. She climbed into the cockpit, studied the panel and the switches, did the pre-takeoff check, and taxied out to the runway, setting her gyro to the runway heading.

After takeoff, remembering Pete Goff's words, she climbed the ship upstairs to gain sufficient altitude before returning to the field to make her takeoffs and landings. When she had plenty of altitude, she slowed the airplane to approach speed, dropped the gear and flaps, and made a practice landing. Then fog started to roll in and she thought she had better get down. Her heading indicator fortunately had not precessed as she had not been up very long. The heading indicator had to be set by the compass and reset every 15 to 20 minutes. When it precessed, it moved away from a correct setting and had to be manually realigned with the compass by the pilot. If the pilot neglected to do this, she would fly an off-course heading — a dangerous situation.

Teresa was in such a hurry to get down that she made a bouncy landing.

> In fact, it stunk! I had too much flying speed, so I was forcing it down, and I was over-controlling on the rudder. It was a very light aircraft with that in-line Rolls engine in it, and had a narrow gear compared to the P-47. I was used to the P-47 sitting right on the runway once you chopped the throttle. My P-51 landing wasn't so great since I jack-rabbited down the runway, but at least I got in through the fog.

The weather closed the field that day. The next morning, she had two more landings to finish and went over to Operations and told them she had only one landing in the airplane. But the Ops Officer said, "You're checked out, be on your way."

So Teresa flew to Ft. Myers, Florida, stopping on the way at Palm Springs, California; Tucson, Arizona (due to mechanical difficulty); El Paso, Midland, Abilene, and Houston, Texas; Mobile, Alabama; and Jacksonville and Bartow, Florida. She met stormy weather in Texas so extensive that she made short hops from one base to the next as she found breaks in the overcast. Unfortunately, she did not have her uniform jacket and so was not allowed in the Officers Clubs. Her meals were sandwiches grabbed in base Canteens.

Teresa's main problems during this trip were not connected with the airplane, but with creatures that kept her from getting a good night's rest. At the base BOQ in Palm Springs, a scorpion crawled across the floor near her bed. The morning of her departure at Tucson, she found a snake coiled up next to the P-51's tire. Even though the crew removed the snake, as she navigated, she worried about the possiblility of another one somewhere in the cockpit. And, finally, at her destination in Bartow, Florida, where she spent the night, she saw roaches so big, "You could throw a saddle on them. My worry wasn't about flying — it was about the crawly things keeping me from sleeping."

The P-51 Mustang was fun to fly after all the trips in the P-47 Thunderbolt. The P-47 engine was so big that the pilot had to zig-zag across the country to

Betty Gillies about to ferry a P-47 at NCAAB.

see where she was going. There was no forward visibility, because the nose was always riding above the horizon. And, on takeoff, the pilot had to look out at a 45 degree angle — she couldn't see down the runway during a P-47 takeoff or landing. But the P-51 was different; she could see where she was going and it was light:

> It was a sweet airplane; I just loved the P-51. You could fly close formation. . . . It was one of my favorite aircraft.

When Teresa arrived at Ft. Myers, an AT-6 was waiting to be taken to Seattle, Washington.

> I criss-crossed the country in the same clothes. On the way back I met Barbara Erickson in Dallas, Texas. She was on her way back to Base in Wilmington. So I said, "Barbara, could I borrow your

Betty Gillies.

blouse?" We were both the same size. "And do you have an extra pair of pants?" Well, she let me borrow the blouse.

Betty Gillies had suggested that "wherever you went, if they have a double mattress, take your pants off and smooth them out, and put them in between your mattresses and lie on them."

Teresa's trip ended with taking a P-39 from Oklahoma to Great Falls, Montana, and then a P-47 back to NCAAB. It had been 4 weeks, 17 states, 6 aircraft, and 11,000 miles!

You should have seen my hair, my pants, and my shirt, after what was supposed to be a "short" trip.

I never believed the Air Forces after that. They were short of pilots, and it was always a hurry-up thing. But there was one time I remember that really frosted me. Towards the end of 1944, I recall having to pick up an A-24 in Texas and take it to Aberdeen, Maryland. I had so much trouble with that plane mechanically that it took several days to make the trip. I couldn't get the gear up, so had to stop and have that fixed, after I had to pump it down. And, then the radios went out, so I stopped at another base. Next, I couldn't get the bomb-bay doors closed. On the final leg of that flight, as I was approaching Aberdeen, exhaust fumes poured into the cockpit and I had to request a straight-in approach for an emergency landing. They cleared me . . . and I had to land with the canopy open and the wind blowing in my face. It was hard to see the exact height above the ground. As my wheels touched the runway, the Control Tower operator said "that was a beautiful landing." I replied, "You ought to see me grease them in when I'm not applying my lipstick." I was really relieved to get that plane to its destination.

I walked into Operations to get my Memorandum Receipt signed for that aircraft. I told them how much trouble I had getting it there in one piece. The officer replied, "Well, no wonder, it's a Class 26 airplane."

I said, "What's a 'Class 26?'"

The officer responded, "The next few days they will taxi it out to the area of the Aberdeen Proving Ground used for bombing practice and pilots will find out how accurate their air strikes are."

Teresa was furious. They had not told her what kind of airplane she was going to fly, nor that after all her trouble they were going to put it out in the middle of the Proving Grounds and have BT-13s strafe the thing to see if they could hit it!

Later Teresa found out that planes were marked with either a red diagonal or a red cross to indicate flying status.

Planes marked with a red diagonal I would fly, but never a plane marked with a red cross. That red cross meant that something mechanical was definitely wrong with the airplane. A red diagonal meant something minor was wrong, like radio problems, or it would miss occasionally. But a red cross meant you weren't supposed to fly it.

But the women pilots weren't told. Teresa recalls:

I was one of the lucky ones, really. With some of the COs around, you could hardly say "go take a dive." I was really careful from that day on. When I went through that Form 2, I read it carefully. I would not fly one with a known, serious deficiency. But I had flown them, not knowing, and that was bad. . . . I don't blame other pilots for refusing to fly them.

Standing, pilots Cecilia Hunter and Emily Heister listen to Teresa James and Gert Meserve compare notes while waiting for a C-60 at Newark Army Air Base, New Jersey. James recalled "We had a military airline. We used to pick up pilots coming back from delivering planes. We used to pull engines on each other all the time with passengers in the back. They didn't know if it was real or not. We stayed real proficient so people in back couldn't tell."

The first fast transport Teresa flew was a Lockheed C-60 Lodestar — a beautiful, stable, and easy aircraft to fly. The transition to the larger planes,

Teresa's 1944 Crew Chief of the C-60, Sergeant Rosenbloom, Newark, New Jersey, who flew the pilots back to Farmingdale.

Aircraft Arrival Report.

according to Teresa James, was never difficult; there were just more throttles and gauges.

Aircraft Arrival Report.

In December 1943, Teresa had orders to take a C-60 to Patuxent Naval Air Station on the Chesapeake Bay in Maryland. Her crew chief, Sergeant Rosenbloom, had to fix a minor malfunction before takeoff, so Teresa waited in Operations drinking coffee.

> After a lengthy delay, we finally took off. It was a two-hour flight, so I knew I'd need the ladies' room the minute I got down. Well, I had a tough time getting into Patuxent. Arriving at my destination I called the Tower and identified myself as the Army C-60 and asked for clearance to enter the pattern. I circled at 2,000

feet. Patuxent, a cluster of three fields, bordered on a military danger area from 0 to 5,000 feet, which made me a little paranoid.

In between my repeated requests for an acknowledgment, I listened to the Tower barking weird instructions: "Angels, one point five, repeat, Angels one point five, break out!" My head was on a swivel looking for phantom traffic — then another voice screamed: "Chicken in the rough, chicken in the rough, take it around, take it around." I was ready to request an emergency landing for a critical bladder condition, when the Tower operator barked: "To the Army plane calling the Tower, enter the traffic pattern at 1,500 feet and report downwind." I made a combat approach and greased the wheels on the runway. The tailwheel didn't hit the tarmac until the last intersection, where I met the "Follow Me Jeep."

I taxied behind him to the parking area, killed the engines, and left that C-60 without any explanation to the crew chief. I was in a fast trot as I entered the Operations building.

I impatiently inquired the location of the Ladies Room. One of the personnel behind the counter said, "The head's on the upper deck." That's like telling me nothing, so I said again, "Where is the Ladies Room?" Maybe the guy in Ops did it deliberately, but anyway, he told me it was on the second floor.

I took the steps two at a time, pushed through the first door on the right while trying to wiggle out of my flight suit, and headed toward the commode slamming the door behind me. Wow! I made it! Oh blessed relief! For the umpteenth time I'm swearing off coffee before flight time!

After a few minutes I heard the outer door open. I hurried in case the next girl was as desperate as I to go to the bathroom. I flushed and was still pulling up my flight suit as I exited the commode. I was startled to see a guy at a urinal.

So I learned from the Navy, "a head" is not a head, it's a latrine.

In her haste to leave the C-60, Teresa had forgotten to bring in the copies of the Memorandum Receipts, so she walked back out to the airplane where one of the linemen was talking to her crew chief.

He didn't know whether to salute or say hello to me. I smiled and said, "Hi." And then I asked him about the strange instructions from the Tower — the chicken in the rough, take it around bit. He smiled and said, "Oh, that's the pilots in the F4-Us [Corsairs] practicing carrier landings." I thanked him for enlightening me.

Teresa got the Memorandum Receipt from the map case in the C-60 cockpit and started back towards Operations where she had to get it signed by the CO or the adjutant to show that the plane was delivered to the Naval Air Station.

> I dreaded going back to Operations. As I opened the door I heard a voice, a real Southern drawl, say, "Well, change my oil; it's a girl." I could feel ten sets of eyes boring into my back as I approached the counter. There, sitting at the Duty Officer's desk, was the guy I had encountered in the latrine. "Well, if it isn't the head hunter!"
>
> I requested the brash CO to sign the receipt for the plane, which he did, promptly handing it back. He offered transportation to the Mess Hall for me, my co-pilot, and my crew chief. I replied, "I don't have a co-pilot."
>
> He was surprised: "No co-pilot in a twin-engine?"
>
> I sounded a little sarcastic when I told him it didn't take two pilots to up the landing gear and lower it. But he didn't like my retort, and asked, "Who's your CO?"

Two days after the incident a directive came out — no more flying twin-engine aircraft without a co-pilot.

> I was surprised because what did you need a co-pilot for in a C-60? Maybe you needed one in a C-47 to take care of a few radio details, but you really could fly it by yourself. But try and convince those desk-flying dummies.
>
> I preferred the C-60 over the C-47. It was more stable in my opinion. I loved the C-60. I could really wind that sucker up.

Gert Meserve, Nancy Batson, and Teresa were the three women who flew the C-60s to pick up pilots and take them to their bases. The shuttle operation was called "Snafu (situation normal, all fouled up) Airlines." Referring to the C-60, Teresa said,

> That aircraft had wonderful control and great stalling characteristics. We used to try and see who could land the shortest on the runway, loaded or empty. We could always make the first intersection to turn off the active runway. . . .
>
> When I was flying a C-60, I would pick up 10 to 20 pilots at their delivery point and return them to their home base. At Mitchel Field on Long Island, New York, a bunch of guys back from overseas were awaiting transportation to different bases. They put the ones

who were going to New Castle and Baltimore on our airplane. I'm sitting up front in the left seat and Gert came up through the aisle as a guy got off the airplane and went into Operations. The only reason I knew it was because the Crew Chief came through and said "We're minus a passenger — he went into Operations." I kept waiting and finally decided to go into Operations and find out where that joker was.

The young Captain was telling the Ops officer that he didn't go through this war and live, just to come home and get in an airplane flown by some female who would kill him. The Operations Officer told him: "Listen, she has more time in one year than you had all the time you were overseas — she's a safe pilot, so you get back on the airplane." And he did.

They sent him to New Castle Army Air Base to ferry airplanes and he and I became good friends. He said he was sorry for the remark he had made. Only once or twice had he heard, while he was overseas, that they had female pilots flying airplanes, and he had never seen a female pilot before. So, he got a little uptight and upset, and I really can't blame the guy.

Gertrude Meserve Tubbs remembers:

Teresa and I flew the Lodestar; we took turns. Teresa would usually win the landing contest. She could turn off at the first intersection. It was a little tricky but she did it. She probably used the brakes, and she had to land right at the edge of the runway.

"Snafu Airlines" operated as a military airline up and down the Atlantic Coast, but mostly it had the Newark run.

We used to call it the up-and-down milk run. A whole bunch of pilots would leave Farmingdale and go to Newark. We would pick up pilots who had just dropped off P-47s and haul them back to Farmingdale to get another batch going. I used to call in "Newark Tower, how are you? How about clearing me in on 22?" I did it all the time — I could get away with that stuff.

Teresa's most exciting ride happened when she was a passenger. It was 12 May 1943, on a flight from New Castle Army Air Base to Farmingdale in a C-60 with pilot, co-pilot, and 17 ferry pilots aboard. Immediately after the ship left the ground, it assumed a stalled attitude. Teresa reported later to the Director of Flying Safety:

Teresa James, Gertrude Tubbs, and Helen Richey (the first female co-pilot for Pennsylvania Central Airlines after the war).

From where I sat, I could see the co-pilot at the controls and noticed he had the control column in full forward position. I observed the pilot trying to correct the [nose-up] attitude by making a stabilizer adjustment. An order was given for everyone to come forward, in an attempt to correct for tail heaviness. The change of weight and balance after the passengers moved forward caused the ship to assume a normal flying attitude. One pilot moved some chutes which were under the seats to the front of the ship. Everyone returned to their same seats for the duration of the flight.

Teresa said the problem was caused by sandbags that were used in the back of the C-60 for transition training:

... And then we came along and put our parachute bags on top. It was really stupid. I've never seen a plane in that attitude without it stalling out. It could have killed us.

On another C-60 trip, when Teresa was also a passenger, the Army pilot overshot the runway at Hagerstown, Maryland. According to Teresa, he overshot the runway and was braking it, so he "groundlooped that sucker."

> We didn't have enough runway to take off, and next thing I knew, I'm looking right down this mountainside. There was a steep drop-off at the end of the runway. The tail was hanging over the end and I could see a thousand feet down. He had to drag it up with both engines wide open, which scraped the belly of the airplane. We were lucky.

On another ferry trip during the summer months, Teresa and Helen Richey were in two P-47s. They had on flying coveralls over their uniform pants and shirts and parachutes over this. The pilot fit snugly into the cockpit with no room to spare. On this day the two girls were flying pretty close formation but with all sorts of gyrations. Teresa called Helen, the leader, on the radio telephone (R/T) and asked if she was OK and what was the matter with the airplane?

Richey replied, "Dammit Jamsie, I'm trying to get out of this damn chute and coveralls so I can get my pants down. I've got to go so bad I'm ready to bust. I'm going to indoctrinate the relief tube." The relief tube was a hose device with an oval-shape tunnel especially designed for a man's urinal.

After about five minutes of mad scrambling through the skies with Teresa in hot pursuit, Richey's plane finally achieved level flight again. Teresa heard her laughing uproariously into the R/T, shouting, "Mission accomplished."

When they landed at the next refueling stop, Teresa made Richey tell the ground crew she had used the relief tube. It didn't take long for that story to travel through the Air Forces. The girls were questioned many times: "How can you gals use that thing?"

Teresa said that later on Helen told her she had lots of practice on relief tubes when she was flying for the British Air Transport Auxiliary in England during the early part of the war, prior to joining the WASPs.

Helen Richey was a delight, a great pilot. She loved people, especially screwballs who told wild and mysterious tales that she would repeat without urging. She was a feminine aviation pioneer from McKeesport, Pennsylvania, and a close friend of Amelia Earhart, with whom she often flew. During her service with the ATA, Helen had been the first woman to fly the Hawker Hurricane fighter. She had been left in charge of the American contingent of pilots in England when Jacqueline Cochran returned to the United States.

In the 1930s, Helen had set many flying records. She was the first woman in Allegheny County, Pennsylvania, to earn a pilot's license at the age of 19. In 1933, Helen and Frances Harrell set an endurance record, staying in the air 237 hours and 43 minutes. In 1936, Helen set an international women's speed record for light planes, covering 100 kilometers in 55 minutes. That same year, she established the women's world altitude record for light craft by reaching 18,000 feet. Helen Richey was the only woman to train Army pilots. After the war, she was the first woman pilot on a regularly scheduled airline. (She had a job as an airline co-pilot in 1933, but this ended abruptly when she wasn't allowed to join the Airline Pilots Association.)

She was attractive, submissive, and spiritually minded. She was photogenic and petite — just a bit over five feet tall. In 1942, from England Ernie Pyle wrote in one of his columns:

> Helen is 33 now, and as engaging as ever. She wears a dark blue uniform with the wings of ATA on her tunic. The uniform has slacks for flying and skirt for street wear. She looks very snazzy in her outfit.

Born in 1909, Helen died at the age of 37, apparently a victim of an overdose of sleeping pills. She was quoted as saying, "When a girl reaches 37, her flying days are over."

On another flight out of the ordinary, Teresa and Helen Mary Clark picked up P-47s at Republic Aviation on Long Island for delivery to the 336th Fighter Group in Wilmington, North Carolina. After takeoff, Teresa noticed Helen Mary's plane bobbing up and down. She tried to call her on the VHF radio, but Helen Mary didn't acknowledge. She was still climbing for altitude when Teresa pulled into tight formation from where she could see Helen Mary fumbling around the cockpit.

> We had been flying for awhile when I noticed smoke in the back part of her airplane. I again flew as close to her as possible and pointing to her tail, I mouthed the words "smoke," and she shook her head up and down acknowledging like she understood me.

Teresa then looked at her map to find the closest military airport. It was Bolling Field, Washington D.C. She called the Control Tower and told them she was flying alongside a P-47 without communications, with smoke pouring from the rear of the airplane. The Tower operator advised her, "Return to your point of origin — do not land; we have no repair facilities here." Teresa replied, "You'd better clear the area, we're coming in."

Once again, Teresa flew as close as possible to Helen Mary's plane and pointed down to let her know they had to land. Helen Mary acknowledged, thinking there was something wrong with Teresa or her aircraft. She followed Teresa in for the landing, and the fire equipment followed Helen Mary's smoking plane down the runway. She pulled off to the side, jumped out, and

To Theresa + Jemmy —
A real gal — fun to be
with! Someday I'd like
to race you across the
continent. How about it?
Love,
Del

Adela Scharr checking out in a P-39.

finally realized that it was her own airplane that was in trouble. It turned out to be an electrical fire, hence, no communications. When she had left Long Island, she had trouble getting her gear up, and she thought all the time that Teresa had been trying to tell her that the gear wasn't up.

Helen Mary Clark had learned to fly in 1934 using her own aircraft. She was

Women ferry pilots picking up P-39s at the Bell factory, Niagara Falls, New York: Betty Archibald, Nita Bolish, ___ Jordan (Danville, Virginia), Rita Wilkes, and Janet Zuchowski.

married to W. Gerould Clark, a well-known polo player and real estate broker, who, although not a pilot, was supportive of his wife's flying. Helen Mary was quiet, charming, and dignified with a shy smile, golden brown hair, and freckles. Flying her own plane out of Englewood, New Jersey, she had her two sons in the air before they were four, and both became accomplished pilots at a very young age. In 1942, when she was one of the first five women to join the WAFS, her sons were nine and twelve years old. After joining, Helen Mary had very little time for home life. During the last three months of service in 1944, she never had a day off. But whenever she had a flight to Newark, near her home, with a fighter or big bomber, her husband would meet her and drive her home for a short visit — in most cases four hours.

Helen Mary ferried fighters, medium-attack bombers, and heavy transports from production plants to their assigned fields or ports of embarkation. On one occasion, the P-38 she was flying away from the Lockheed plant at Burbank burst into flames. She whipped the twin-engine fighter around and headed for the field. Fire trucks raced her down the runway as she landed, shooting chemicals at the burning plane, and the fire was out before she stopped.

On another "thrilling" flight, the plane's engines went dead at 10,000 feet over Texas. She made a forced landing without damage to the plane.

Adela "Del" Scharr also had an extra chance to prove what women could do. When some of the commissioned officers refused to fly the P-39 Airacobra, Headquarters had to do something, so the Colonel asked Del to fly it. The Army gave her five hours in an advanced trainer to get used to more speed, then she flew five hours in a difficult twin-engine aircraft as a step towards the P-39.

There was no ground school for the P-39, so Scharr's only preparation for flying the Airacobra was a short film put out by the Bell Company. She got the instruction booklet that came with the plane and memorized it, so she would know blindfolded where everything was located in the cockpit. Next she made up her own procedures to follow. She then checked herself out in this single-engine, single-seater which introduced many novel features. Its 1,150 hp Allison engine was situated behind the cockpit, in the center of gravity, and large fuel tanks were directly under the cockpit. It had a 37mm cannon mounted in the nose, six Browning machine-guns, and featured a nose wheel and car-type cockpit doors.

Del Scharr spent days practicing takeoffs and landings, perfecting new techniques. She found out that the men had not been landing the P-39 fast enough to avoid stalling. The plane was difficult to fly because the pilot constantly had to reposition the center of gravity by shifting the fuel load from one tank to another. And, the plane had a nasty high-speed stall when the aircraft lost lift and it went out of control if the pilot didn't take prompt, corrective action. If the Airacobra was doing 300 mph and the pilot pulled back sharply on the stick, it would stall. Scharr said, "It was a real caricature of an airplane." She later checked out several other women in the P-39.

Scharr flew P-39s from Montreal to Los Angeles with stops in between. Some were shipped to Britain, so that pilots there could train on larger aircraft. Others went to Great Falls, Montana, where they were picked up by Russian pilots. And, indeed, almost half the P-39s produced went to the Soviet Union.

Because so many men had accidents training in the P-39, by December 1943 a pursuit training school for the aircraft was set up at Brownsville, Texas. There properly trained students learned that the aircraft, like the B-26, was not as vicious as rumors and under-trained pilots had made it appear.

During her time flying for the Army Air Forces, Del Scharr logged time in many types including the P-39, P-47, P-51, B-17, B-24, and B-25. She earned the nickname "Madame P-Shooter" because of her safety record in the P-39. Actually, none of the women who flew them had accidents in the P-39.

After some of the women checked out in the P-47, P-51, B-25, and B-26, they would be sent to one of the bases where male pilots were having difficulty flying that type aircraft, and that bit of psychology worked.

Teresa said,

> The guys quit cracking them up. I know from my own experience that at a base in South Carolina pilots were having takeoff and landing accidents in P-47s. I delivered a P-47 there and they made a big deal out of a woman flying "The Jug" as it was called.

Teresa claims that there were no more accidents in P-47s.

"You fly your airplane; don't let it fly you," were choice words of wisdom. There were hazards involved, but Teresa explained:

> We never thought about them. We just thought about things as an incident. Years later looking back, what a hazard! But back then, you just got out there and flew. You did what you were told. I guess we thought we were doing something real terrific for our country.
>
> The difference between flying then and today — well, it was like owning a 1920s Ford and owning a . . . Cadillac [of today]. You have everything at your fingertips now. Back then, we were the Air Forces' guinea pigs. When a WAFS pilot climbed into a cockpit, she had no way of knowing if the plane was constructed perfectly, or if some small, but serious, defect had been built into the plane. You didn't know if everything was OK, you just hoped and prayed. We were honest-to-God test pilots.

Chapter 8

Ten Grand

The fact that Teresa was one of several WASP pilots based at Farmingdale, Long Island, New York, the seat of the main Republic factory, gave her some special benefits. One was that she flew many P-47 Thunderbolts or "Jugs," as they were popularly called. Another was that she was around when the official photographer was taking pictures. But perhaps most of all, she was there and next up on the roster in 1944 the day they rolled out the 10,000th Jug built. And she was the pilot designated to fly it to Newark, New Jersey.

So Teresa James, the girl from Wilkinsburg, Pennsylvania, became a special part of Thunderbolt history and a member of the P-47 Pilots' Club.

That 10,000th P-47 rolled off the line on 20 September 1944, the product of the "Racers," as the workers at Farmingdale were called. The first P-47 had been delivered to the Army on 18 March 1942.

When Republic began producing the Thunderbolt for the Army, the working force was made up of 5,000 employees. As output jumped to keep pace with Army requirements, Republic increased its work force to 24,450, over half of whom were women. Production efficiency increased as the Army Air Forces put pressure on Republic. In filling the Army's first order for 773 aircraft in 1942, the average working hours to produce Thunderbolts were 22,927 man/woman hours per ship. By 1944, when the 10,000th rolled off the line, it had dropped to only 6,290 hours.

The efficiency in production was reflected in costs; omitting government-furnished equipment such as engines, guns, radios, etc., the average initial cost of $68,750 (in 1942 dollars) decreased to $45,000 by the time the

Getting ready to christen *Ten Grand* at Republic Aviation, Farmingdale, Long Island, New York, are Marianne Nutt, Gertrude Meserve Tubbs, Teresa James, Helen Richey, Betty Gillies, Lt. Joe Tracy, Jacqueline Cochran, Mr. Marcher (President of Republic Aviation), Gwen Cowart, Helen Deitweiler, and Liz Pearce (in back).

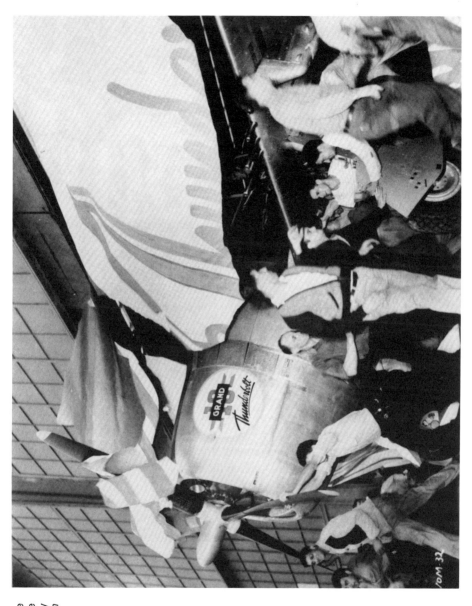

"The Big Push." After the christening, the tug rope broke, so Republic factory personnel had to push *Ten Grand* out to the ramp.

Under Secretary of War Robert P. Patterson at the christening of *Ten Grand,* at Republic Aviation, New York.

10,000th P-47 was produced.

With such a record of achievement, the War Department was happy to present Republic Farmingdale Division the Army/Navy Production Award for the third time.

On 22 September 1944, *Ten Grand,* as the aircraft was called, was about to be rolled through a paper curtain and out of the hangar door for delivery to the Army. The entire Thunderbolt workforce was invited to share the festivities. It already had been test-flown.

The Mitchel Field band led a march around the buildings past the enthusiastic applause of the crowd. All of Republic's day-shift of "Racers" followed onto the field east of Building 17. There speeches were given, workers pulled the famous aircraft — and then the rope broke! The aircraft had to be pushed out in front of the speakers' stand before the Army and civilian guests. Waiting to greet the plane in front of the hangar and the celebrity-thronged grandstand was one of the most famous women pilots and chief of the WASP, Jacqueline Cochran. Standing on a lift-truck platform, she smashed a bottle of champagne over the propeller hub, and the plane was moved back, ready for Teresa.

Ten Grand was in the Army. The Republic workers had reached a milestone

The *Ten Grand* departs. Teresa James taxies out to the runway at Republic Aviation, Farmingdale, New York, for takeoff to Newark Army Base, New Jersey, after the aircraft was christened by Jackie Cochran.

in production, fulfilling with this 10,000th aircraft what was only a dream in 1940 and an untried experiment in production when the Japanese had attacked Pearl Harbor on 7 December 1941.

A ten-man ground crew gave the aircraft a final check, preparing it for departure. And Teresa James was ready for her role in the day's events. After posing for pictures, she climbed into the cockpit and taxied to the duty runway. As *Ten Grand* lifted off the ground, en route to Newark Airport, it was on its way to war.

Before leaving the fighter at Newark, where it would be put on a ship to go overseas, Teresa wrote a note in the log book, to be read by *Ten Grand's* first combat pilot.

Along with other Jugs, *Ten Grand* was shipped to Liverpool, England, where the aircraft were lifted onto lorries (trucks), and driven to their final destination. Some of the Jugs were towed to their bases, which wasn't easy. Even though the rudders were removed, the truck drivers had to know the height of every bridge on the route and the width of every street because even with the wing tips removed, the Jugs cut a wide swath. The mechanics would put the planes in flying condition in 50 hours.

Ten Grand's first assignment was to the 79th Fighter Group of the 12th U.S. Army Air Force on the Italian Front, where it was first flown by the Group Commander, Colonel Gladwyn E. Pinkston. The Colonel returned from a test hop and praised the plane highly, as did other expert combat pilots who had a chance to fly it.

Actually, the plane hardly could have found a better group to take it into combat. The 79th Falcons were referred to as "America's busiest fighter-bomber sideshow." The veteran outfit had been in six campaigns — Egyptian-Libyan, Tunisian, Sicilian, Italian, French, and Northern Italian. In constant and savage combat, the 79th had flown the roughest, toughest, most perilous of all Air Forces assignments — close-support fighter-bomber. The Falcon Group had flown with three Allied Air Forces — the Desert Air Force and the United States 9th and 12th Army Air Forces. It had flown close-support for the ground troops of four Allied Armies — the First, Fifth, Seventh, and Eighth — under every manner of field conditions from 47 different air bases.

During the Western Desert days, the Group flew under the British, wore British battle dress, ate British rations, lived in British tents, and moved in British lorries. War correspondents often referred to the Falcons as "Monty's Pets," as the celebrated British military chief spent many hours with the Group, which served as a forward base for his personal plane.

The versatility and power of the P-47 Thunderbolt can be appreciated after a casual glance at the Group's records. The Falcons were the first to pin 2,500 pounds of bombs to the wings and bellies of the aircraft for use in actual combat missions. When the 12th Air Force was entrusted with supporting the

At a 12th AAF P-47 base in Italy, Lieutenant John F. Martin (later Colonel) from Culpeper, Virginia, and Tom Drummond, Republic Aviation Corporation technical representative, pose before *Ten Grand*, the 10,000th P-47 Thunderbolt built by Republic. This was the plane in which Martin flew the 30,000th sortie flown by the 12th Air Force 79th Fighter Group, the famous "Mosquito Fighter Group" in more than two years of fighting in the Mediterranean theater of war. (Photo, AAF)

Army's landing on the beach-head in southern France, the 79th Fighter Group's P-47s were the first planes over the assault beaches on D-Day, 6 June 1944.

The Group was the first to sink a warship with the P-47. The aviation world was astounded when eight Thunderbolts, flying from a base in Corsica, fired on the 30,000-ton aircraft carrier *Aquila*, formerly the luxury liner *Roma,* as she lay in Genoa Harbor. The 79th was the first 12th Air Force unit to strafe Germany proper from France.

Ten Grand arrived at the Falcons' advanced fighter-bomber base a few days before the flight of the epic 30,000th combat sortie of the 79th Fighter Group. It was primed immediately by crack 12th Air Force ground crews to make the milestone run.

Ten Grand received its baptism of fire and made its combat debut on 19 January 1945, when it flew out with the sensational Falcon Fighter Group on that 30,000th sortie. The target was in the Causewar Area north of Ravenna, and the snarling Thunderbolts went in low to smash roads despite heavy concentrations of anti-aircraft fire. The pilot, Colonel John F. Martin, from Culpeper, Virginia, then Commanding Officer of the 79th, brought *Ten Grand* back from the run as clean as it had gone in. After the war, Colonel Martin was lost while flying a P-51 out over the Atlantic. He was in the Air Guard of one of the southern states at the time.

After its first sortie, *Ten Grand* was assigned to Lieutenant Arthur E. Halfpapp, a 24-year-old pilot of the 87th Fighter Squadron, 79th Fighter Group, who, in combat missions over the shaggy terrain of the Mediterranean theater, already had won an Air Medal and a Distinguished Flying Cross. When Lieutenant Halfpapp looked over the record for the P-47, he found the note written on the flight report by WASP Teresa James:

> To the pilot of *Ten Grand*: You hit the jackpot. May every mission be a Grand one and every chance a winner! Good Hunting!

Shortly thereafter, Lieutenant Halfpapp wrote to Teresa, who had left her address along with the note in the aircraft logbook:

February 7, 1945
Italy

Dear Miss James,

Just a few lines to let you know I received your note and have been the lucky guy to receive *Ten Grand*. It is a swell ship but we had a little trouble with it and it took twenty hours of flying to find out it needed an engine change. On my first mission I took off with a thousand pound bomb and it cut out once for me. I completed that mission and when I came back I told my crew chief that it ran rough and vibrated a lot. That got me a new prop and they fixed one plug that was not firing. On a couple of other missions it acted as if it was going to cut out, so I got the engineering office on the ball and they found out that there was a bad bearing in the engine and the whole oil system was full of filings.

The plane handles like a dream in the air and it's too bad that had to happen to the engine. I had one strafing mission with it and it pulled me out of a few very tight spots. The plane I had before was a D-23 Razorback and the best one in the outfit and I sure hated to lose it. I only have 57 missions to my credit so far and I have been overseas nine months now. I first started flying from Corsica and most of my missions were in Italy and France. I was very fortunate to get in on the invasions of Southern France and later on move over there. We then stayed there for awhile until we got the sad news that we were coming back to Italy. Now we are in Italy on the Adriatic side flying with the British. I don't think I ever want to see Italy again once I leave it.

As much as I hate to admit it, I have never seen any Jerry aircraft in the air. That is, not close enough to get a shot at them. We have gotten plenty of them on the ground, but we just can't get them to come up in the air. It is a lot of fun flying over here and I can say we don't run into as much flak as bombers do, but they still shoot at us on every mission. I think I talked too much about myself already, so I'll ask you a few things now.

How about telling me about the type of work you are doing and also a few of your flying experiences! Do you fly very often and what do you think of the Thunderbolt? Do you fly any other planes besides the P-47? It will be very interesting to me to find out some of these things, so how about dropping me a line telling me about your flying and yourself. I'll be waiting to hear from you, so drop me a line when you aren't too busy.

Yours,

ARTHUR E. HALFPAPP

P.S. Everyone calls me "Art" for short.

Lt. A.E. Halfpapp   0-820485
79th Fighter Group 87th Fighter Sq.
APO 650 c/o Postmaster

The other pilots who later flew *Ten Grand* in combat were Lieutenant James McGovern, Lieutenant Charles Gregory, and Lieutenant Harold Wuest. McGovern also flew the aircraft when it was assigned to the 87th Squadron of the 79th Group. In a letter to the P-47 Thunderbolt Association he said:

> It was my misfortune to get it punctured full of holes on our last two dive bombing missions. But my roommate, Lt. Charles W. Gregory of Danville, Kentucky, did a more complete job. He managed to fly the old indestructable "Jug" home to base from somewhere south of the Alps to Cesenatico, Italy, with two cylinders shot away, and oil all over the outside.

Ten Grand survived the war. The battered Jug, still with the 79th Group, was assigned to occupation duty in Linz, Austria. Lieutenant Wuest, one of the pilots who flew it at Linz noted that "it had had two sets of wings and needed another — there were about 148 overlapping patches on the top side of the wing." When half the Squadron's planes were sabotaged with rocks in the air intake scoop, the impeller blades in the turbo were sheared off and *Ten Grand* crashed. However, it was patched up once more, and like many other P-47s, made its final flight to Kassel, Germany. At the base there, the surviving P-47s were lined up on the ramp. Hand grenades were tossed in each cockpit, one at a time, to destroy the once gallant Thunderbolts, now war surplus.

Chapter 9

D-Day Plus Forty

Teresa's husband, Dink, had sent her an invitation to his graduation, Class 43-H, at Stockton, California. "I was too busy flying to go," she remembers. His first assignment was Roswell, New Mexico, where he became a B-17 instructor, and Teresa was able to visit him there when she made a trip to the West Coast.

In the early part of 1944, Dink got word that he was to be shipped overseas. After volunteering for this duty, he was given a 48-hour pass when he got to New Jersey. Betty Gillies gave Teresa a pass as well.

In Europe, Dink joined the 337th Bombardment Squadron which had been activated on 15 July 1942, assigned to the 96th Bombardment Group. When Dink arrived, he was stationed at Snetterton Heath, England, flying B-17s in the European Theater of Operations. Campaigns for this Group included the air offensive in Normandy, Northern France, Rhineland, and Ardennes-Alsace. Teresa wrote to him frequently.

Dink was on his 13th mission on that fateful day of 22 June 1944 when his B-17 was shot down. Coincidentally, his last letter to Teresa was postmarked the same day. He had written it the day before:

To: Teresa James Martin
      2nd Ferrying Group
      N.C.A.A.B.
      Wilmington, Delaware USA

Dear "Butch"

How are you getting along, honey? Are you still working hard and doing a lot of flying?

We're really keeping busy over here and I'm not fooling, I'm tuckered out. If these jerks would quit shooting at us, it wouldn't be bad, I think they're mad at us though.

I had a close one on takeoff yesterday morn. I was loaded to gross and we had a 400 foot ceiling. It was still dark yet and the place was really closed in. I just got into the murk and good and solid in a climbing turn on the gauges when the horizon went out. I rolled right out of the turn and went on needle, ball and airspeed and stayed on them till I broke out on top, wheh! what a sweat. Bill, my co-driver turned about 40 colors when it went out, some fun. This place is just like a place I was instructing at.

How are you getting along with the gauges, honey? Are you driving on them yet or not? Learn all you can about them honey, they're the best insurance in the world, next to a flak suit.

I still haven't received any mail at all, it has been 2 ½ months since I've had any. It's plenty lonesome . . . not getting any mail when we get home. I'd sure appreciate a letter about now. I don't know what's holding it up. I feel like a stinker, all I do is eat, sleep and fly. I haven't even had time to take a bath for a couple of days.

Enough griping now, I'm tired now. Still love me as much as ever, honey? I love you more than anything in the world honey and I always will. I miss you more every day and can't wait till this mess is over and I can get to see you again.

I'm going to grab some rest now, write soon.

Forever,

"Pop"

Lt. George L. Martin   0-753906
337th Bomb Sqdn. 96th Bomb Gp.
APO 559 c/o Postmaster, NY, NY.
(postmarked Army Postal Services 587 A.P.O. USA 22 June 1944)

Teresa was ferrying P-47s out of Republic Aviation's field in Farmingdale, when she received the dreaded telegram notifying her that Dink was MISSING IN ACTION. She got leave and went back to Pittsburgh, but Betty Gillies called her and said she was needed at the base, so she returned to Delaware. "I was better off flying and being with the girls," she said.

Time passed and Teresa got no further word on Dink's missing status. One day, Helen Richey suggested that she would write to her old buddy, Jimmy Doolittle, to see if he could help. The information he sent her, dated 28 November 1944, reiterated that Dink was the pilot of the missing B-17 which other members of the mission claimed was hit.

HEADQUARTERS EIGHTH AIR FORCE
Office of the Commanding General
APO 634

28 November 1944

Miss Helen Richey, WASP
NCAAB
Wilmington, Delaware

Dear Helen:

Thanks for your note of 30 October received the other day. It was good to hear from you and to learn that you are well. Sorry to hear that your little flock is being disbanded. What have you in mind now?

We have very little information on Lt. George L. Martin. Here's what we have. He was listed as missing in action on a bombing mission 22 June. His plane was hit and No. 3 engine caught fire. Immediately after the ship was hit it went out of control and three chutes were seen by crew members of other planes to open. Shortly thereafter, the airplane leveled off and four more chutes were observed to come out. It is impossible to say whether the last three got out or not as the ship went out of sight soon after this. While we have heard nothing further, you can see from the above that there is a good chance that George got out and is now a prisoner of war. Should we receive any more dope I will pass it on at once. Mrs. Martin will get some measure of comfort from the knowledge that George was very well liked by his associates, was doing a swell job and had made substantial contribution to the cause for which we are all fighting. Please extend to her my sympathy and hope that George may yet show up.

Had Ernie Pyle out to the house for supper a short time before he went home. He is a great little guy and did a magnificent job over here. Should you see him give him my kindest regards and tell him we are all looking forward to the time his health will let him come back.

Sincere best,

As ever,
J. H. DOOLITTLE
Lieut. General, USA

JHD:G

That week, in November 1944, Teresa saw a picture in the *New York Daily News* with the caption, "American Airmen Captured by Nazis." A side view of one of the men in the picture looked like her husband, with two of his crew members whom she had met prior to his volunteering for overseas duty. This left her with the assumption that he was a POW and would come home after the war was over.

When the WASP was disbanded in December 1944, Teresa returned to Pittsburgh to work in her parents' flower shop. Having received no further information from the Army regarding Dink, she wrote to the Chief of Burial Records in the European Theater asking if in fact her husband was deceased. He replied that there were no records to substantiate the death. On 26 July 1945, however, she received a letter from Lieutenant General Ira Eaker, extending his sympathy in the official determination of the death of her husband.

HEADQUARTERS, ARMY AIR FORCES
Office of the Commanding General
Washington 25, D.C.

July 26, 1945

My dear Mrs. Martin:

With deepest regret I have learned that an official determination has been made of the death of your husband, Second Lieutenant George Louis Martin, who has been missing in action since June 22, 1944, in the European Area.

Lieutenant Martin's excellent record at Stockton Field has been brought to my attention, and it gives evidence of the earnestness and diligence with which he performed his work as an aviation cadet. After receiving his commission he quickly established the reputation of being a skillful, courageous pilot, his good judgement and indomitable spirit winning the admiration of those who served with him.

I realize nothing I can say will compensate for the loss of your husband, but I hope your grief will be alleviated to some extent by the memory that he made the supreme sacrifice for his Country's cause.

My heartfelt sympathy is offered to you and to other members of the family in behalf of General H.H. Arnold, Commanding General, Army Air Forces, who is temporarily away from Headquarters.

Very sincerely,

IRA C. EAKER
Lieutenant General
U.S. Army Deputy Commander
Army Air Forces

Mrs. George L. Martin
Ferry Command Pilot
Hotel Huntington
Huntington, New York

* * * * * * * *

HEADQUARTERS
US THEATER GRAVES REGISTRATION SERVICE
THEATER SERVICE FORCES
EUROPEAN THEATER

GRSC (Rear) APO 887

30 August 1945

Pfc. George Wertheimer
505 QM Car Co USFET
APO 757 U.S. Army

Dear Pfc. Wertheimer

Reference is made to your recent inquiry in regard to the place of interment of Lt. George L. Martin, 0-753906.

At the present time we have no record of the death or burial of Lt. Martin. To further verify his casualty status, it is suggested that you direct your inquiry to AG Casualty Division, HQ TSFET, APO 887.

Yours very truly

PHILIP J. WOLF
Capt. QMC
Chief, Burial Records Division

On 29 March 1949, Teresa was notified that her husband's remains were initially interred with his comrades at Solers, France, and would be casketed and shipped to Jefferson Barracks National Cemetery in St. Louis, Missouri. Following this letter was one signed by Major General Edward Witsell informing Teresa that her husband was a crew member on a B-17 which crashed in Joinville-le-Pont, France, hit by anti-aircraft fire on a mission to Paris.

In 1950, while she was working in the flower shop, a man came in and asked for Teresa James Martin. He identified himself as the waist gunner on her husband's plane. After she collected her wits, Teresa asked him what had happened that day. He remembered the hit that blew off the whole front end of the plane. He said that her husband, his co-pilot, and the navigator never knew what hit them. His last memory was jumping out of the wounded bomber and his chute opening. His memory loss lasted many years, but, said Teresa, "He had to find me to tell me the story. He said he was going on to New York, but he would return so we could talk some more." But the man never came back.

> I still felt that my husband was alive and would come walking in
> some day. The Air Force told me his supposed remains were buried
> in St. Louis with his crew, but somehow, I didn't believe it.

In 1984, when Teresa learned that Paris, France, was chosen as the reunion site of the P-47 pilots, she started to search through all her old papers and World War II correspondence. She found the name of the mayor of Joinville-le-Pont and its distance from Paris. She wrote to the mayor who then contacted the President of the Veterans Association in that area. They both extended an invitation to Teresa to visit, and asked her to let them know when she would be available.

Teresa had also written to Levon Agha-Zarian, a flamboyant British-

American ex-RAF pilot who flew P-47s over the Hump during the Burma Campaign. Agha-Zarian, who was the first President of the P-47 Thunderbolt Association, was then living in France. He wrote to Mayor Gibout, then to Teresa:

> We are a group of World War II fighter pilots. There are 3000 of us with a very few lady pilots. Colonel Teresa James is one of them. She has some documents which show that her husband crashed in your area during the last War. As she will be the guest of the Armee de L'Air in May or June 1984, she'd like to come and visit you. After our telephone conversation I am sure she will be welcome and everyone will be delighted to meet each other. It will be very nice on your part to write her about this accident and all the people that remember it. We'd like to get the name and address of the family which helped the survivors of the Bomber 17 to escape. And also we'd like to know where the others have been buried.
>
> Teresa is our "Jacqueline Auriole." She is a very nice lady, not sophisticated at all. No one will imagine what she has done except if they had the opportunity to see what we have seen.
>
> Sincerely,
>
> AGHA-ZARIAN —
> P-47 Thunderbolt Association

Dear Terry:

There are people in Joinville-le-Pont who saw your husband George crash. One of the crew may have escaped, was hidden and raised in the town. The name of the road has been changed to a resistance leader. Have spoken with the authorities — they await your visit.

All this can be arranged for you and your friends when you are over here. The town is only about ¾ hour from Paris. What imparts is that they are proud of you and [of] all [that] certain worthwhile Americans did for them.

As for you and your other WASPs like in all doings we men do not know what we could do without your feminine help.

Suggest you write them direct in English — tell them to write you in French. You can get somebody to translate (confidentially, we can get Decoration of the French Resistance who saved and hid any of us).

My love to all of you,

Agha
Box 183
Nice CDX 06006
FRANCE.

The first letter Teresa received from Monsieur le Maire Guy Gibout, Mayor of Joinville-le-Pont, in 1983 was in French, so she took it to a travel agency to have it translated. He had asked her to contact him when she got to France, but by the time Teresa arrived, he was no longer Mayor.

Teresa had received another letter from a Frenchman dated 23 April 1983 (translated):

Dear Madam:

Thank you very much for your letter and excuse me for not answering it sooner. Since Mr. Agha-Zarian and yourself sent me all this information, I have been in touch with different organizations of veterans in the area. I can already tell you that I have found some people who witnessed what happened.

I am myself President of the l'Union Francaise des Associations de Combattants de Joinville-le-Pont. This is an association of veterans from Joinville-le-Pont and we have organized a meeting and some people are now working to get all the information we need about your husband. We will let you know what's going on but I can already tell you that we will be very happy to receive you in our town when you will be with us in 1984. If you have any mail to send me please send it to the following address under my name and hoping to hear from you very soon.

Sincerely yours,

Roger Belbeoch
5 Rue Hippolyte
34340 JLP France

P.S.   A veteran from the French Resistance.

When Teresa learned that the French had found witnesses who had seen her husband's plane crash, she remarked,

> Needless to say, I was astounded. This now had become a three-fold trip. While overseas I would be looking up my deceased mother's childhood home in Ireland, try to visit all the shrines in France, and go to Joinville-le-Pont, in addition to our P-47 reunion, of course.

Before leaving the States, Teresa wrote Roger Belbeoch, the Veterans Association President, and set a date to go to Joinville-le-Pont. There was one small problem, she said. "He speaks no English, and I speak no French." Agha-Zarian, who had compared Teresa to Madame Auriole, the famous French lady pilot who had set all the speed records, had told Teresa not to worry. "We'll just take you out to where your husband crashed."

On Sunday, 27 May 1984, the French Mother's Day, Roger Belbeoch and his wife, accompanied by an interpreter, met Teresa at her hotel in Paris at 9:00 in the morning. Teresa recalls,

> I didn't know what to say when I met him. Such a dumb way of conversing. At that point in my life I was so sorry that I never took a language in school.

They drove to City Hall in Joinville-le-Pont where Mayor Pierre Aubry gave Teresa a welcoming speech in English, with many people milling around.

> I saw a plaque "IN MEMORY OF GEORGE L. MARTIN" and a piece of B-17 landing gear in a niche as I walked by, and I thought, how interesting that they have kept that.

The Mayor introduced Teresa to the witnesses of the crash.

> We got in a car with a caravan of people following and drove out to Avenue de Lille, the crash site where all these people came from. We pulled up in front of the house that the wing had hit. The woman who was living there during the war still lives there (she's now in her 80s). Through an interpreter I talked to this dear lady who said she was in her house when the plane crashed. She described to me her feelings about the crash and how it was a miracle that the plane stayed in the middle of the narrow street.
>
> On the wrought-iron fence in front of the house is a memorial plaque with the inscription in French "IN HONOR OF THE NINE

AMERICAN AIRMEN WHO GAVE THEIR LIVES FOR FREE-
DOM JUNE 22, 1944." I was overcome with sadness. All I could
think of was Dink's last letter, which bore the same post-mark, and
I went through this emotional thing that was overwhelming. Just
then 2 young girls, about 14 years old brought me a large arrangement of red, white, and blue flowers which I placed at the base of
the Memorial with a prayer. The girls spoke to me in French. My
interpreter said they were saying they were so sorry I had to place
the floral arrangement by the plaque.

Then we walked over to the garage where two 17-year old boys
hid when they heard the air raid siren back in 1944. They heard the
crash moments later, and when they peeked out the door, they saw
the smoking wreckage and a body lying between two trees. The
body was intact. They rushed him to the hospital, but he was
already dead. That man was my husband. The neighbors ran into
the street and gathered pieces of bodies before the Germans
arrived. They were later taken to Church for blessing, and then
buried together.

Teresa asked why nothing had changed over 40 years' time. She was told
that the people in France don't move, they don't change, they just stay in the
same place. Even the trees were still there where the boys had picked up the
body. As Teresa stood, looking between the trees, thoughts flashed through
her mind:

One of his crew members [had told] me Dink never knew what
hit him — the whole front of the plane blew up — and it wasn't true
at all.

For 40 years Teresa had not known what had happened:

It was awful. I never went through anything like that — standing
out there and looking at that . . . street, and knowing Dink, and
how he flew, to try and save lives. . . . You wouldn't believe how
narrow that street is, and I couldn't help thinking what a tremendous job he did, even though the bomber was crippled. And he
saved all those townspeople who were hiding in the houses on both
sides. To me it was a miracle how he got that plane down. Most of
the houses had little fences in front. The right wing hit a house, but
only took out part of the fence, that belonged to [the] dear lady that
I met and talked to . . . and she told me what a wonderful way my
husband put the aircraft down without something catching fire.

The two Frenchmen who, as boys of 17, pulled George Martin's body out of his B-17. Teresa James met them 40 years later in France. (Courtesy of Teresa James)

> How he kept it from slamming in, and how he kept it going straight,
> is something I'll never know. He was such an excellent pilot.

The area around the town was built up, and there was really no field for an emergency landing as Joinville-le-Pont was a suburb of Paris. Yet it was still exactly the same when Teresa James stood there, as when Dink's B-17 had crash-landed. He had had very little means of maneuvering.

Teresa had never expected that she would meet anyone who saw her husband's crash, especially the two teenage boys who had picked up his body. In 1984, they were 57 years old. Later she found out that all of the activity involved with Dink's crash had saved the Joinville-le-Pont bridge from being blown up.

Escorted by the Mayor, Teresa was taken back to City Hall, followed by the crowd of villagers. In the assembly room, with the witnesses to the crash sitting in the front row, the Mayor made presentations in French, and then in English. The two former teenagers who had found Martin's body presented Teresa with another exquisite floral bouquet. Knowing that she was a florist, they had gone out of their way to present an impressive arrangement.

Next, a man presented Teresa with a gold coin on a red velvet background in a 10- x 12-inch frame. An attached letter read:

> It was on 22 June 1944 towards 7 p.m. The weather had been fair, and I was 17.
>
> As was so often the case in those troubled days, we suddenly heard the sound of sirens. A few minutes later the German guns began to shoot against a B-17 squadron.
>
> Because of the heavy fire, my father decided to ask our neighbor, a friend called Mr. LeGoff, to share his shelter. On our way we stopped in the garage to avoid being hurt by shell splinters. Then, suddenly, we heard a very loud noise like that of a high-speed train.
>
> Before we could realize what was going on, we could feel a terrible blast, immediately followed by a violent explosion. I popped out, still shocked by the noise. A few yards away, under a privet hedge, the corpse of an American aviator was lying. . . . After he was transferred to the Hospital of Cretell, my father examined the impact [area], where he discovered a unique coin.
>
> He then kept it in his purse for the rest of his life, like a talisman. After he died in 1965, I decided to save this relic and kept it with me until today.
>
> Now I am happy and proud to see that the City of Joinville-le-Pont and its Mayor, Mr. Pierre Aubry, venerate this hero and his friends. This coin is now going back to his family as a testimony of his sacrifice for freedom in the world.
>
> Signed:
> JACQUES DUME
> 27 May 1984

When Mr. Dume presented Teresa with this coin, he spoke to her through an interpreter. Another lady presented Teresa with a framed picture that she had taken of the crash. Another witness had a piece of metal from the bomber mounted in a blue-velvet lined box. Still another had a dog-tag belonging to a crew member; another had the B-17 manufacturing plate from the instrument panel.

> They also presented me with a tea-cup size gold medal from the City of Joinville- le-Pont, inscribed: GEORGE MARTIN, June 22, 1944.
>
> It really touched me, seeing the piece off that airplane and the picture of the crash. It got to me. . . . After not knowing for 40

years, and after those letters from the War Department, to think that I would meet the people who discovered my husband's body. It was uncanny. I was so amazed. . . . I could hear my heart pounding in my own ears. I wanted to thank these people but I just stood there and cried and cried. I couldn't say a word. I felt like such a dope. It was awful. I could just visualize him trying to get the B-17 down that narrow street between the houses, averting real tragedy as far as the townspeople were concerned.

Mayor Aubrey's wife took Teresa by the arm and led her into another room, followed by the many witnesses. There they had prepared an elaborate champagne brunch in her honor. Teresa remembers,

I finally calmed down, with the aid of a few sips, and collected my wits. I thanked about 50 people, kissing cheek to cheek.

I was sort of emotionally charged anyway. I had just come from my first visit to Ireland to see where my mother had lived, and now this. Later at a posh restaurant we were served a seven-course dinner. I was happy, tired, and emotionally drained when they drove me back to Paris. At last I know now what really happened to my husband.

Teresa wrote about her feelings of that day, as she was on her way back home to West Palm Beach, Florida:

We had just taken off from De Gaulle Airport and as we were climbing for altitude, I gazed through misty eyes at Paris below. I wondered if my husband ever saw the city when he flew over it — or was it always cloud-covered?

. . . I remember when he learned to fly at the airport where I was a flight instructor. We both had two loves — each other and flying.

World War II separated us when he joined the Army Air Forces. . . . His letters were full of concern when he learned I was about to fly the same type of aircraft he had been flying, though I reassured him that I wouldn't have problems as long as the wings stayed on.

I survived the war years, but my husband didn't. I never was sure what really happened to him, until a stroke of fate took me to a little town in France.

Sunday, 27 May 1984, was "a day to remember," Teresa says, an "incredible event that . . . ended 40 years of uncertainty."

Chapter 10

Disbanded and Postwar

Even though the WASP pilots began by ferrying light aircraft, by the time the program ended, the women had ferried 77 different types, including the P-40, P-47, P-51, C-47, C-46, B-17, A-25, A-26, B-25, and B-29. Of the 1,830 WASPs who had been accepted, 1,074 graduated. These women and the original WAFS logged more than 60 million miles flying for the Army Air Forces.

Yet in spite of all of their accomplishments, the WASP program came to an abrupt end on 20 December 1944. General Henry H. "Hap" Arnold had addressed the last WASP class to graduate on 7 December 1944, acknowledging that the women were 100 percent instrument (blind flying) rated, 98 percent twin-engine rated, and 80 percent single- and twin-engine fighter rated. In addition, he noted that five women were qualified on all types of aircraft, including four-engine bomber and transport planes, and even though no more than 303 WASPs had been assigned to ATC, they had delivered a total of 12,652 aircraft. By September 1944, he added, they had been delivering three-fifths of all pursuit ships coming off the assembly lines.

> . . . I am glad to be here today to talk with you girls who have been making aviation history. You and all WASP have been pioneers in a new field of war-time services, and I sincerely appreciate the splendid job you have done for the AAF.
>
> You, and . . . your sisters, have shown that you can fly wingtip

to wingtip with your brothers. If ever there was a doubt in anyone's mind that women could become skillful pilots, the WASPs dispelled that doubt.

The possibility of using women to pilot military aircraft was first considered in the summer of 1941. We anticipated then that global war would require all our qualified men and many of our women. We did not know how many of our young men could qualify to pilot the thousands of aircraft which American industry could produce. There was also the problem of finding sufficient highly-capable young men to satisfy the demands of the Navy, the Ground Forces, the Service Forces, and the Merchant Marine. England and Russia had been forced to use women to fly trainers and combat-type aircraft. Russian women were being used in combat.

In that emergency I called in Jacqueline Cochran, who had herself flown almost everything with wings and several times had won air races from men who now are general officers of the Air Forces. I asked her to draw a plan for the training and the use of American women pilots. She presented such a plan in late 1941 and formed the basis for the Air Forces' use of WASP.

Frankly, I didn't know in 1941 whether a slip of a young girl could fight the controls of a B-17 in the heavy weather they would naturally encounter in operational flying. Those of us who had been flying for twenty or thirty years knew that flying an airplane was something you do not learn overnight.

But, Miss Cochran said that carefully selected young women could be trained to fly our combat-type planes. So, it was only right that we take advantage of every skill which we, as a nation, possessed.

My objectives in forming WASP were, as you know, three:

1. To see if women could serve as military pilots, and, if so, to form a nucleus of an organization which could be rapidly expanded.

2. To release male pilots for combat.

3. To decrease the Air Forces' total demands for the cream of the manpower pool.

Well, now in 1944, more than two years since WASP first started flying with the Air Forces, we can come to only one conclusion — the entire operation has been a success. It is on the record that women can fly as well as men. In training, in safety, in operations, your showing is comparable to the overall record of the AAF flying within the continental United States. That was what you were called upon to do — continental flying. If the need developed for

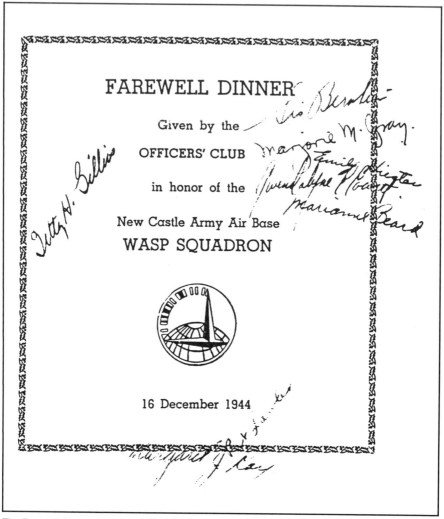

The *Farewell Dinner* program, 16 December 1944, given in honor of the New Castle Army Air Base WASP Squadron.

Opposite: The "last supper," 19 December 1944. Front row, l to r: Mary Russo, Virginia Clair, Helen Richey, Betty Gillies, Nancy Love, Josephine Pitz, Helen McGilvery, and Nancy Baker; second row, _____, Anna Flynn, _____, Jill McCormick, Janet Zuchowski, Virgie Jowell, Sis Bernheim, Gwen Cowart, and Mitchell Long; third row, Dorothy Coburn, Gert Tubbs, Ruth Anderson, Celia Hunter, Helen Mary Clark, Virginia Alleman, and Ruth Adams; back row, Teresa James, Grace Birge, Sarah Pearce, Marge Gray, Esther Poole, Jane Straughan, Maggie Ray, Nancy Batson, Rita Moynahan, and Marianne Beard; behind Beard, Avanell Pinkley, Emily Heister, Eunice Oates, Rosalie Grohman, and Mrs. Margaret Anderson.

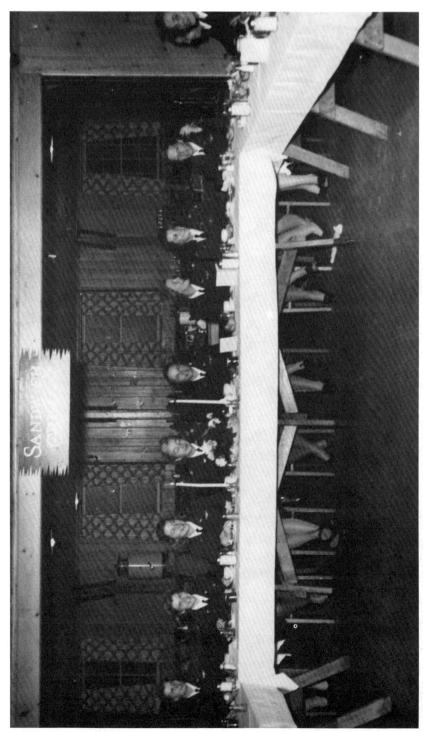

The "last supper" had been held 19 December 1944: at the head table, l to r, Gertrude Meserve Tubbs, Helen McGilvery, Nancy Batson, Nancy Love, Betty Gillies, H. M. Clark, Teresa James, and Sis Bernheim Fine.

On 20 December 1944, at the Republic Aviation factory, the WASP's were officially demobilized. L. to r: Jackie Cochran, Helen Deitweiler, Marianne Beard Nutt, Helen Richey, Gwen Cowart, Liz Lundy, Teresa James, Gertrude Meserve Tubbs, and Betty Gillies.

SQUADRON MEMBERS

Ruth Adams

Ruth E. Anderson

Nancy L. Baker

Nancy E. Batson

Marianne I. Beard

Kathryn L. Bernheim

Grace P. Birge

Virginia Clair

Helen Mary Clark

Dorothy R. Colburn

Gwendolyne E. Cowart

Irene G. Davis

Anna L. Flynn

Betty H. Gillies

Marjorie M. Gray

Rosalie L. Grohman

Virginia L. Hagerstrom

Emily Heister

Celia M. Hunter

Teresa D. James

Florence E. Lawler

Mitchell I. Long

Jill McCormick

Helen S. McGilvery

Marian G. Mann

Alice L. Middleton

Rita J. Moynahan

Euncie S. Oates

Sarah E. Pearce

Avanell Pinkley

Josephine Pitz

Esther D. Poole

Margaret J. Ray

Helen Richey

Mary M. Rosso

Betty Scantland

Jane S. Straughan

Gertrude S. Tubbs

Joanne Wallace

Virginia A. Whisonant

Mary C. Wilson

Janet J. Zuchowski

Margaret M. Anderson, House Mother

WASP Squadron Members at New Castle as listed in the *Farewell Dinner* program.

women to fly our aircraft overseas, I feel certain that the WASP would have performed that job equally well.

Certainly we haven't been able to build an airplane you can't handle. From AT-6s to B-29s, you have flown them around like veterans. One of the WASP has even test-flown our new jet plane.

You have worked hard at your jobs. Commendations from the generals to whose commands you have been assigned are constantly coming across my desk. These commendations record how you have buckled down to the monotonous, the routine jobs which are not desired by our hot-shot young men headed toward combat or just back from an overseas tour. In some of your jobs I think they like you better than men.

I want to stress how valuable I believe this whole WASP program has been for the country. If another national emergency arises — let us hope it does not, but let us this time face the possibility — if it does, we will not again look upon a women's flying organization as experimental.

We will know that they can handle our fastest fighters, our heaviest bombers; we will know that they are capable of ferrying, target towing, flying training, test flying, and the countless other activities which you have proved you can do.

This is valuable knowledge for the air age into which we are now entering.

But please understand that I do not look upon the WASP and the job they have done in this war as a project or an experiment.

A pioneering venture, yes. Solely an experiment, no. The WASP are an accomplishment.

We are winning this war — we still have a long way to go — but we are winning it. Every WASP who has contributed to the training and operation of the Air Forces has filled a vital and necessary place in the jigsaw pattern of victory. Some of you are discouraged sometimes. All of us are, but be assured you have filled a necessary place in the overall picture of the Air Forces.

The WASP have completed their mission. Their job has been successful. But as is usual in war, the cost has been heavy. Thirty-seven WASP have died while helping their country move toward the moment of final victory. The Air Forces will long remember their service and their final sacrifice.

So, on this graduation day, I salute you and all WASP. We of the AAF are proud of you; we will never forget our debt to you.

Thinking of that fateful day, Teresa recalled:

I remember it like it was yesterday when I walked out that gate. I stood there with the same emotion as when they found Dink. Something died right there. After flying for 27 months with the women like you were sisters, flying around the country and then coming back and chatting about it — just like a big family, and then all of a sudden you lose that. How could you go home to people who didn't understand? You became part of each other because you could talk about what happened, the scary moments, and bolster each other. You became very close, and all of a sudden this association has ended. A letdown like this is bound to create a

A reunion of those who lived in BOQ 14: standing, housekeeper A. J. May, Jill McCormick, Esther Rathfelder, Dorothy Fulton, Barbara Poole, Teresa James, Sis Bernheim Fine, Gertrude Tubbs, Ruth Adams, Kay Brick, and Marge Gray; seated, Marianne Nutt, Nancy Love, Mrs. Anderson (housemother, known as "Andy"), Betty Gillies, Helen Mary Clark, Magda Tache, Bill and Jerry (Helen Clark's sons), and Avanell Pinkley.

problem for a lot of people. There was a great deal of alcoholism afterwards — you had to get lost in something.

Fortunately for me my parents had [the] family flower business, so I got lost in work. I felt sorry for the girls who didn't have families to go back to. I can really identify with Vietnam veterans coming back. At least we had recognition when we came back.

I was devasted when we were disbanded. I tried to get into the Chinese Air Force. They wrote me a nice letter saying they didn't need pilots. I tried the airlines and they all told me the same thing — public opinion wouldn't permit a female pilot in the cockpit, even if she had a four-engine rating. So, I went back to flight instruction, but there were very few students after the war. Private aviation was at a low ebb.

Nancy Love had said that women were physically and temperamentally suited for fighter operations:

They are smaller and thus more comfortable in a tiny, crowded cockpit. They are quicker to react and are supposed to have a lighter, more delicate touch, and thus are better able to surmount emergencies when they arise.

Looking back on the WASP record, they definitely have proved that women are useful in military flying and can replace men for combat. The theory that women can't take it physically has been thoroughly disproved. I have it in writing from excellent authority, that women's physical record is equal to, if not better, than men's over a two-year period.

Asked about her postwar plans on that 20th of December, Nancy Love laughed — a laugh without much mirth. "I have none," she said. "I'm leaving today, flying a C-54 (four-engine transport) to California. Going to fly all night and think about what has happened to me . . . and to us. . . ."

Another WASP, Gerri Bowen (Olinger), later remarked, "When our service was disbanded, I was heartbroken, devastated, and really missed the flying. After all, I couldn't ask the Army to rent me a bomber for an hour of pleasure flying, now could I?"

During the first two postwar years, Teresa attended the Benz School of Floral Artistry in Houston, Texas, and then the Hinson School of Design in Cleveland, Ohio. Her parents opened a second flower shop in Wilkinsburg, Pennsylvania, which Teresa managed, handling all the floral designing.

Teresa still went to the airport weekends, hoping to pick up a few students, even though the pilot market was saturated and not many people were learning

Teresa James as WAF Director with the 375th Troop Carrier Wing, Air Force Reserve, around 1953.

to fly. She bought a Piper aircraft.

> Piper was going great guns. I flew evenings and when I wasn't designing floral arrangements on Saturdays, when most of the weddings were held.

Teresa was commissioned a Major in the Air Force Active Reserve in 1950 at Jacksonville, Mississippi, and served until her retirement in 1976. She started with the 375th Troop Carrier Wing in Pittsburgh as a recruiter and Special Services Officer. She served at the 2253rd Air Force Reserve Combat Training Center from 1951 to 1953. From 1953 to 1960 she was Special Services Officer for the 375th Troop Carrier Wing at the Greater Pittsburgh Airport.

From 1961 to 1965 she was assigned to the 5040th Air Base Group Alaskan Air Command, Elmendorf Air Base, Anchorage, Alaska. She spent four years on the Red Carpet Committee, meeting visiting dignitaries — she once went on a sled-dog ride with Tex Ritter. She also received several commendations for casualty assistance while working in Family Services.

While Teresa was in Alaska, she met Vice President Richard Nixon and his

Graduation from Officers Training School, Orlando, Florida, 1944. L to r: Helen Mary Clark, Teresa James and Irene Gregory. (Courtesy of Teresa James)

wife, Pat. Mrs. Nixon and Teresa got to talking about ancestors. Pat said her family was from Ireland. Teresa's grandmother was a Branigan and it turned out that Pat Nixon also had a Branigan in her family. Thinking they were possibly related, they promised to correspond. Teresa was anxious to trace their ancestry back, as both Branigans came from the same part of Ireland. She later received a gracious letter from Mrs. Nixon in January 1961.

Teresa also renewed the acquaintance with Jacqueline Cochran while she was in Alaska when Cochran made a trip there looking for land to purchase. Teresa's good friend and well-known bush pilot, Jo Edwards, got a job as Cochran's co-pilot and secretary.

Cochran had wanted the WASP to be militarized. In fact, early in 1944, when passage of a bill to do this seemed imminent, it was decided to send women to the Army Air Forces Tactical School at Orlando, Florida, to prepare them to become Army officers as they had been promised when they signed up. Unfortunately, the bill to give them veteran status was killed.

For years after the war, Teresa kept up the fight for recognition of the WASP pilots as veterans.

Teresa James giving instrument instruction in a simulator at Allegheny County Airport, Pittsburgh, Pennsylvania, after World War II. "As before the war, when I first started to fly, after World War II I never flew in mannish clothes, always in high-heels, which I kicked off inside the plane," remembers James. (Courtesy of Teresa James)

I wrote to all the Congressmen on my own. I bombarded everyone who came in the flower shop with petitions.

I found out one person can do a hell of a lot if you've got the time and some bucks for postage. I was ticked off at the injustice of the situation. The guys who were stuck here in this country were afraid we would take their jobs and they would have to go overseas. They weren't really stuck; all those instructors just wanted to stay here.

One day, Jacqueline Cochran called Teresa about the pending legislation. She told Teresa she had worked for years for the same thing, yet with all her contacts still couldn't influence it. She was not very encouraging, and it was not a very successful conversation.

That evening, Cochran called Teresa again to suggest a meeting to see if she

In 1954 Teresa James looks at a tree she had planted in 1943 at NCAAB. (Courtesy of Teresa James)

could help. Teresa felt that Cochran's assistance couldn't do her any harm, but she also felt it couldn't help her either. In the end, WASP recognition was not achieved until 1977.

From 1966, until her retirement ten years later, Teresa was attached to the 9536th AFRES Squadron at Greater Pittsburgh Airport. She never used her married name as she had not changed her name in August 1942, when she and Dink were married. Before she joined the WAFS, however, she had told Betty Gillies about the marriage.

Teresa also was active in civilian aviation after World War II. In 1950, at the two-day "All Women's Air Maneuvers," she won the initial heat of 75 hp to 125 hp race — fixed gear — on a triangular course at Palm Beach International Airport. In addition to winning the $500 First National Bank prize, Teresa also won the $50-prize for the spot-landing competition with a Piper Pacer, with the spot set in a circle not much larger than the plane. Teresa also entered the Montreal to West Palm Beach Powder Puff Derby, flying with Viola Gentry.

In 1939, Teresa had joined the Ninety-Nines, the International Organization of Women Pilots, and had become a lifetime member. In 1986 she was honored by inclusion in the Ninety-Nines Forest of Friendship in Atchison, Kansas.

September 1963, l to r: Teresa James, Jackie Cochran, and Jo Edwards, Teresa's good friend and Cochran's copilot and secretary. (Courtesy of Teresa James)

Teresa is also a life member of the P-47 Thunderbolt Pilots Association. She belongs to the Order of Fifinella, The Grasshoppers (Women Pilots Association of Florida), the Silver Wings Association, the Florida Race Pilots Association, and the OX-5 Association. Her first P-47 reunion was in Dayton, Ohio, in 1970.

Teresa was awarded a Pancho Barnes Award in 1980, at the 21st Annual Silver Wings Aviation Event at the Coral Gables Country Club, for her contributions to aviation. Silver Wings is a worldwide organization of pilots who made their first solo at least 25 years ago. Two pilots, one male and one female, are selected each year on the basis of their contributions to aviation.

Teresa donated her WAFS uniform to the National Air and Space Museum of The Smithsonian Museum in Washington, D.C., where it remains on display. Her helmet, goggles, and other WAFS items are on display at the New Castle County Airport (formerly the Greater Wilmington Airport and New

Winter uniform, 1960s.

Castle Army Air Base), in Delaware. On 22 July 1985, when the Delaware Chapter of the Ninety-Nines held a Dedication at New Castle Air Force Base honoring the women ferry pilots, Teresa was there in her Air Forces uniform to unveil the Plaque in front of a large audience of dignitaries while TV and radio reporters recorded the proceedings.

In 1988, Teresa appeared in the U.S. Air Force hour-long documentary commemorating the 40th anniversary of the Air Force. The segment on the birth of the WAFS featured Teresa, mentioning how she overcame "a paralyzing fear of flight" to go on to "airborne heroics that would help save America."

Teresa James in an Alaskan parka in preparation for the 1963 Powder Puff Derby Race. (Courtesy of Teresa James)

Teresa in College, Alaska, *ca.* 1960. Flying was "too cold this day." (Courtesy of Teresa James)

Teresa James and Captain Melody at Elmendorf AF Base, Anchorage, Alaska. (Courtesy of Teresa James)

Major Teresa James retired from the USAF Reserves in 1976. She is pictured here at Elmendorf AFB, Anchorage, Alaska, in 1964. (Courtesy of Teresa James)

Checking out in a T-38 in 1965 with Captain Melody of the 317th Fighter Interception Squadron at Elmendorf AFB, Anchorage, Alaska. (Courtesy of Teresa James)

Teresa James, 9536th ARS, Greater Pittsburgh Airport, Pittsburgh, Pennsylvania. (Courtesy of Teresa James)

Lord Louis Mountbatten and Teresa James at the P-47 Reunion at the Royal Air Force Club, London, England, 1947.

Teresa James (on sled) and Tex Ritter (behind, right) dog-sledding in Bethel, Alaska, 1962. (Courtesy of Teresa James)

Epilogue

The WAFS and WASP pilots were very much a part of American history. They were part of the whole movement of women into war work to free men for other tasks. At the same time, they were the victims of male resentment that this was happening. Women pilots were treated in about the same way that the Army had handled Negro (as they were then called) physicians. And yet, the women pilots were very representative of traditional American womanhood, and many were happy after the war to return to their families.

The sad part of their story was that the WASPs, like Teresa James, were not treated as veterans after having done work equivalent to their male counterparts and that they were unable to continue the work they loved. Because the women were not officially veterans, they could not have access to postwar services to help them through the difficult times — nor did they have the GI Bill.

Teresa James found a place in the USAF Reserve and comfort in the eventually successful fight to get the WASP pilots military recognition as veterans.

THE WAFS

When an organization called the WAFS,
Came to the Post, there were many laughs.
All the men raved and hours were spent,
Discussing the dopes that run our Government.

We knew from the first that we were resented,
By the continued aloofness which the men presented.
For weeks they had noticed we weren't tormented,
And whatever they said, we could not be offended.

With a song in our hearts so light and gay,
We continued on our merry way.
For all we could think of was getting a break,
Trying to help when we knew WHAT was at stake.

Then one day I heard a few nasty remarks,
That the females joined this just for a lark.
And they would soon tire of arising at six,
And going to bed each night with the chicks.

Imagine those females flying a plane,
Why the Army Officials must be insane.

To entrust a girl with a job like that,
When she's probably thinking of a ducky new hat!

Why can't women stay at home,
And leave running the Army to men alone?
Think what will happen with them in the sky,
It just won't be safe for us men to fly.

The first time cross country, they'll no doubt get lost,
And we'll have to find them no matter the cost.
I'll betcha they don't know a map from a chart,
Those silly, dumb females out to get smart.

They even acquired our B.O.Q.,
So, we gave it up without much ado,
As there was nothing left for us to do.
But it's a hell of a trick, I'm telling you!

Well, take it from me, it won't be long,
"Till all those dames will get the gong.
And in our hearts will be a song,
When they go back home where they belong.

Here were the men from all walks of life,
Whose cutting remarks were just like a knife.
And all the things I just overheard,
Left me undaunted, much less perturbed.

I thought to myself, "They're the 90 day wonders,
Whose daily occurrence is six or eight blunders!
All they know about flying is no more than we,
But the EGOTISTICAL man is much better than she."

It's tough we know but we are game,
We'll fight no end to make a name.
Remarks and opinions just egg us on
To win a place where we rightfully belong.

There were a few that were on our side,
And with every rule we intend to abide.
To show them they haven't made a mistake,
By giving us this job which we now undertake.

So, we started out to prove our worth,
While we covered just one little corner of earth.
But to us it gave a very good chance,
To show them that skirts were as good as the pants.

Well, they checked us out in an L-4B,
And the shrugging of shoulders was all you could see.
They no doubt figured that at least two or three,
Would be neatly wrapped around a tree.

The first week was swell and we made several trips,
All without mishap which quieted the drips.
The second was better, complete without fault,
Forms filled out correctly which gave them a start!

The third was wonderful almost without incident,
All you could hear was, "Not even an accident?"
It hurt our pride not one tiny bit,
We knew that someday the hecklers would quit.

The fourth week we flew a PT-19,
Over rough rugged country we've never seen.
At our not getting lost, the boys were amazed,
Another "Mission Completed" had left them dazed.

The R.O.N.'s were first thing in mind,
They always were sent before we dined.
To let them know we were safe that night,
And to keep their hair from turning white.

Our flying ability is proven, I hope,
To the wise guys I'll always remember.
We have a good record, they'll have to admit,
We've flown a long way since September.

— Teresa James —
WAFS, 1943

Index

Compiled by Lori L. Daniel

6th Photo Squadron, 28, 30
8th Air Force, 143
9th U.S. Army Air Force, 136
12th U.S. Army Air Force, 136-138
79th Fighter Group, 136-140
87th Fighter Squadron, 138-140
96th Bombardment Group, 141-142
317th Fighter Interception Squadron, 172
319th Army Air Forces Contract Flying School, 42
319th Army Air Forces Flight Training Detachment, 41
336th Fighter Group, 126
337th Bombardment Squadron, 141-142
338th Fighter Group, 104
344th Air Base Squadron, 102
375th Troop Carrier Wing, 164
2253rd Air Force Reserve Combat Training Center, 164
5040th Air Base Group Alaskan Air Command, 164
9536th AFRES Squadron, 167, 172

— AIRCRAFT —

A-24, 115
A-25, 74, 154
A-26, 154
A-30, 79
A-34 (Lockheed Ventura bomber), 61
AT-6, 42-43, 79, 102, 114, 160
AT-8 (T-50 "Bamboo Bomber"), 42
AT-9, 79
AT-17, 42-43
Aeronca, 19-20, 32, 42-43
American Eagle, 32
Autogyros, 32
B-17 (Flying Fortress), 33, 36-37, 39, 69, 111, 130, 141,
    146-147, 149, 151-155
B-24, 35, 79-80, 130
B-25, 130, 154
B-26 (Martin Marauder bomber), 37, 69-71, 130
B-29 (Superfortress), 35, 38, 71-72, 154, 160
BT-13 (Vultee Vibrator), 42-43, 77, 93, 116
Boeing, 16
Boeing 247, 81
Brunner-Winkle Monocoupe, 32
C-46, 154
C-47 (Douglas), 61, 107, 122, 154
C-54, 35, 163
C-60 (Lockheed Lodestar), 118, 120-124
C-69, 35
Cessna 145, 64
D-23 (Razorback), 139
DH-60X (Moth), 38
DT-19, 177
Dart, 32
Davis Monoplane, 25
Douglas, 16
E-2 (Cub), 23
Enola Gay, 71
F4-Us (Corsairs), 121
FR-1 (Ryan Fireball), 39
Fairchild 24, 37
French Breguet, 19
Great Lakes, 32

Gwinn aircar, 35
Hammond "safety planes," 35-36
Hurricane (Hawker), 56, 125
L2-B (Taylorcraft), 46, 50, 77, 80
L-4, 86
L-4B (Liaison Taylorcraft), 38, 77, 87, 89, 177
L-4MB (Jacobs), 42
Lady Bird, 72
Lockheed Electra, 16
Lockheed Lodestar, 69, 123
Luscombe, 32
OX-5 (Travel Air), xi, 4-5, 12, 14-16, 23, 32, 38
P-38, 79-80, 129
P-39 (Airacobra), 21, 115, 127-130
P-40, 154
P-47 (Thunderbolt, "The Jug"), ix, xi, 39, 79, 86,
    99-104, 109, 111-115, 123, 125-126, 130-131, 134,
    136-140, 142, 146-147, 149, 154, 168, 173
P-47D, 105, 110
P-51 (Mustang), 33, 37, 79, 112-114, 130, 138, 154
P-61 (Black Widow), 39
PT-17 (Boeing Stearman), 62, 89-91
PT-19 (Fairchild), 38, 43, 76, 78, 80, 89, 92-93, 103-104
PT-19A (Fairchild), 77
Piper Cub, 32, 48-49, 64, 83, 89, 103, 164
Piper Pacer, 167
Sikorsky, 19
Spitfires, 56, 102
Stinson, 16, 32, 103
T-38, 172
Taylorcraft, 32, 42-43, 55
Ten Grand, ix, xi, 132-138, 140
UC-61, 63
UC-78, 42
UPF7 (Waco), xi, 32
Waco, 27, 76
Waco 10, 32
Wellingtons, 56

— A —

AAF Memorandum Receipt, 70
AAF Training Command, 69, 71
Aberdeen Proving Ground, 116
A-bomb, 71
Adams, Ruth, 58, 85-86, 106-107, 157, 162
Agha-Zarian, Levon, 146-149
Air Corps Ferrying Command (ACFC), 37, 53, 61, 64,
    145
Aircraft Arrival Report, 119-120
Aircraft Delivery Memorandum, 73, 116, 121-122
Air Forces Medal, 64, 138
Airline Pilots Association, 126
Airmail, 18-19
Air Progress Week, 15
Air races, 36
    National, 37, 95
Air raid siren, 150, 152
Air show, xi, 1-2, 8-10, 12, 15-16, 20, 37
Air Transport Auxiliary (ATA), 35, 125-126
Air Transport Command (ATC), 31, 35, 37-39, 41, 46
    Ferrying Division, 31, 35, 37, 39, 46, 68-69
        Second Ferrying Group, 38-39, 46, 80, 141
Alabama
    Birmingham, 67
    Gunner Field, 67
    Mobile, 113
    Montgomery, 88
    Opelika, 88

Alaska, 85, 165, 170
  Anchorage, 164, 171-172
  Bethel, 173
Alert Room, 26, 55, 58-59
Allegheny Airport (Pennsylvania), 15, 23, 32, 104, 166
Alleman, Virginia "Ginny," 108, 157
Allied
  Air Forces, 136
  Armies, 136
Allies, 45
Alps, 140
America, 136, 169
American, 19, 35, 41, 45, 48, 56, 89, 125, 144, 147, 150, 152, 155, 174
Anderson
  Mrs. Margaret "Andy," 46, 157, 162
  Ruth, 158
Angel, Bill, 2, 4, 6
Aquila, 138
Archibald, Betty, 128
Ardennes-Alsace, 141
Arizona
  Phoenix, 69
  Tucson, 113
Arkansas
  Little Rock, 90
Armed Forces, 38, 69, 75
Armee de L'Air, 147
Army Air Corps Technical School (Mississippi), 28
Army Air Forces Air Transport Command (AFATC), 53
Army Air Forces Tactical School, 165
Army Airport (Louisiana), 87
Army/Navy Production Award, 134
Army Postal Services, 142
Arnold
  Colonel William Bruce (Hap's son), 73
  General Henry H. "Hap," ix, xi, 31, 34-35, 38, 64, 69-70, 145, 154
  George, 31
Atlantic Ocean, 36, 79, 123
Aubry, Mayor Pierre, 149, 152-153
Auriole, Jacqueline, 147, 149
Australia
  Melbourne, 34
Austria
  Linz, 140
Avenger Field (Texas), 41-43
Aviation Enterprises, 41-42

— B —

B-4 bag, 61, 81
Bachelor Officers' Quarters 14 (BOQ14), 46-49, 79, 113, 162, 176
Baker
  Colonel Robert H., 31, 37, 40, 49, 79, 80
  Nancy, 157
  Postal Superintendent, 18
Ball, Clifford, 23
Bally, Lieutenant, 88
"Baltimore Flying Prostitute," *see* B-26
Barnes Award, Pancho, 168
Barnstorm, 19
Batson, Nancy, *see* Crews, Nancy Batson
Batten, Bernise I., 39
Becker Aircraft Corporation, 32
Beech, Walter, 10
Belbeoch, Roger, 148-149
Bell Company, 128-129

Bendix Air Race, 34
Bendix Trophy, 34
Benz School of Floral Artistry, 163
Bernheim (Fine), Kathryn "Sis," 39, 63, 107, 109, 157-158, 162
Bettis Field (Pennsylvania), 6, 19, 32
Bing, Captain Charles, 102-103
Birge, Grace, 157
Bohn, Delphine, 39, 55, 61-62, 66, 90
Bolish, Nita, 128
Bolling Field (Washington, D.C.), 126
Bowen (Olinger), Gerri, 163
Boysen, Eleanor, 65
Braebreeze Airport, 16
Brick, Kay, 162
Britain, 35, 69, 130
British, 102, 136, 139, 146
British Air Transport Auxiliary, 125
British ATA (Air Transport Command), 38, 41
British Women's Volunteer Service, 41
Bronze Medal, 8
Brown, Major Harold, 89
Browning machine-guns, 129
Bucharest, 34
Buffalo Aeronautical Institute (New York), 20-21
Burchfield, Phyllis, 39, 55, 62, 66, 90
Bureau of Air Commerce, 35-36
Burma Campaign, 147

— C —

California, 7, 92-93, 95, 163
  Beverly Hills, 97-98
    Boy's Town, 98
  Burbank, 92-93, 95, 129
    Beverly Hills Hotel, 95, 97
  Burbank Field, 92
  Hollywood, 96
    The Brown Derby, 96
  Long Beach, 42, 64, 111-112
  Long Beach AAB, 61
  Los Angeles, 130
  Palm Springs, 64, 113
  San Diego, 32
  Stockton, 141
"Call for Philip Morris," 95
Calloway, Cab, 97
Camp Davis, 72
Canada, 37, 69, 92
  Alberta, 67
    Calgary, 89
  Montreal, 130, 167
Capital Airlines, 2
Carlson, Mr., 53
Carlson's Tailor Shop, 53
Catholic, 29
Causewar Area, 138
Chinese Air Force, 163
Civil Aeronautics Administration (CAA), 27, 34, 77, 103
Civil Air Patrol, 27-29, 34
Civilian Air Transport Command, 53, 68
Civilian Pilot Training Programs, 49
Civilian Student Pilots, 42
Civil Service, 59
Civil Service Bureau, 37
Clair, Virginia, 157
Clark
  Bill (Helen's son), 162

Helen Mary, 34, 39-40, 46, 57, 78, 80, 83, 126-127,
    129, 157-158, 162, 165
  Jerry (Helen's son), 162
  W. Gerould (Helen's husband), 129
Cleveland Air Races, 15
  Thompson Trophy Race, 15
Coburn, Dorothy, 158
Cochran, Jacqueline "Jackie," 34-35, 41-42, 44, 54, 64,
    68, 70, 125, 132, 134, 135, 155, 159, 165-168
Colorado, 29
  Colorado Springs, 28-30
    Broadmoor Hotel, 30
  Denver, 90
Commercial Transport License, 23, 34-35, 38
Confer, Roy, 19
Cooper, Jackie, 98
Coral Gables Country Club, 168
Corsica, 138-139
County Airport (Pennsylvania), 16-17, 23
Cowart, Gwen, 132, 157, 159
Cox, Charles, 20
Crews, Nancy Batson, 39, 57-58, 62, 66, 78, 90, 122,
    157-158

— D —

D-Day, 138
Deaton, Mrs. Clifford "DiDi," 42
Decca Navigation Systems, Inc., 103
De Gaulle Airport, 153
Deitweiler, Helen, 132, 159
Delaware, 143, 169
  New Castle, 42, 65, 103, 123, 160
  Wilmington, ix, 31, 39-40, 44, 47, 53, 61, 80, 83, 86,
    92, 99, 102, 104, 114, 141, 143
    DuPont Hotel, 44, 92
Demobilization, 72, 159
Desert Air Force, 136
Dietrich, Marlene, 98
Director of Flying Safety, 123
Distinguished Flying Cross, 138
Donahue (Ross), Barbara, 39, 61
Doolittle, Jimmy H., 11, 143-144
Dougherty, Dora, 71-72
Drummond, Tom, 137
Dume, Jacques, 152
DuPont Field, 77
DuPuy, Dick, 63

— E —

Eagle Pass Army Air Field (Texas), 69
Eaker, Lieutenant General Ira, 144-145
Earhart, Amelia, 23, 34, 125
Earhart Women's Open, Amelia, 37
Edwards, Jo, 165, 168
Eglin Field, 71
Egyptian-Libyan campaign, 136
Elmendorf Air Base (Alaska), 164, 171-172
Engines
  Allison, 129
  Continental, 90
  Liberty, 19
  Pratt & Whitney R-2800 Double Wasp, 69
  Rolls, 113
England, 7, 34-36, 38, 41, 56, 69, 79, 125-126, 155
  Liverpool, 136
  London, 69, 173
  Mildenhall, 34
  Snetterton Heath, 141

English, 147, 149, 151
Erdmann, Henry, 42
Erickson (London), Barbara J., 39, 55, 61, 64, 67, 88,
    114
Europe, xi, 80, 141
European theater, 64, 141, 144-145

— F —

Fairchild Aviation factory, 77-78, 80, 92
Falcons, see 79th Fighter Group
Faranicci, Guiseppi, 26-27
Farewell Dinner, 156, 160
Ferguson (Wood), Betsy, 39
Ferry, ix, 32, 34, 36-39, 41-42, 45, 55, 59, 68, 72, 77,
    80-81, 86, 92, 103, 112, 114, 123, 125, 128, 142, 154,
    161
Fifinella, 71-72
Flannagan, Father, 98
Florida, 47
  Bartow, 113
  Ft. Lauderdale, 67
  Ft. Myers, 113-114
  Jacksonville, 113
  Lake Worth, xii
  Orlando, 165
  Pensacola, 94
  Tallahassee, 104
    Dale Mabry Field, 104
  West Palm Beach, 153
Florida Race Pilots Association, 168
Flying Falcons, 12
Flynn, Anna, 108, 158
Fogle, Harry, 2-5, 10, 12, 16
Fort, Cornelia, 39-40, 48-49, 88-89
Fox, Mr., 97
France, xi, 41, 138-139, 147-151, 153
  Hospital of Cretell, 152
  Joinville-le-Pont, 146-149, 151, 152
  Northern, 141
  Paris, 146-147, 149, 151, 153
  Solers, 146
Franks, Captain, 78
French, 147-151
  campaign, 136
  Federal Guardian, 18
  Resistance, 148
French, Lieutenant, 76-77
Fulton, Dorothy, 39, 57, 63, 162

— G —

Garrett, Captain Paul C., 41-42
Gateway to the West, see Bettis Field
Genoa Harbor, 138
Gentry, Viola, 167
George, Major General Harold L., 38
Georgia
  Athens, 92
  Atlanta, 88
  Toccoa, 88
German, 19, 150, 152
Germany, 138
  Kassel, 140
Gibbs Flying Service, 32
GI Bill, 174
Gibout, Monsieur le Maire Guy, 147-148
Giles, Major General Barney B., 72
Gillies Aviation Corporation, 38

Gillies
  B. Allison "Bud" (Betty's husband), 38
  Betty Huyler, 36, 38, 40, 48, 55, 57, 61, 63, 67, 69,
    78-81, 83, 88, 102, 111-112, 114-115, 132-133,
    141-142, 157-159, 162, 167
Gimbel, Bruce, 79
Goff, Edgar P., "Pete," 103, 113
Goodman, Benny, 98
Gosport helmet, 26
Grasshoppers (Women Pilots Association of Florida),
  168
Gray, Marjorie "Marge," 65, 157, 162
Greater Pittsburgh Airport, 164, 167, 172
Greater Wilmington Airport, 79, 168
Gregory
  Irene, 94, 165
  Lieutenant Charles, 140
Grohman, Rosalie, 157
Ground Forces, 155
Ground School, 20
Grumman Aircraft Engineering Corporation, 38-39

— H —
Halfpapp, Lieutenant Arthur E., 138-139
Hammerhead stalls, 10
Harrell, Frances, 125
Hawaii
  Honolulu, 48
  Pearl Harbor, 27, 34, 48-49, 136
    Hickam Field, 49
  Waikiki, 48
Heister, Emily, 109, 117, 157
Heller, George, 10
Hell's Angels, 19
Hinson School of Design, 163
Holburn, Margaret, 69
Hope, Bob, 96, 98
Houston, Walter, 95
Houston Municipal Airport (Texas), 41
  Hughes Field, 41-42
Hump, 147
Hungary, 24
Hunter, Cecilia, 85, 107, 109, 117, 158

I —
Icicle Lane, 92
Idaho
  Boise, 55
Illinois
  Belleville, 107
    Scott Field, 107
  Chicago, 2, 4, 6, 22
Immelman, 26
Indiana
  Evansville, 111-112
  Indianapolis, 107
Instrument Flight Rules (IFR), 61
International Organization of Women Pilots, 34, 167
  Ninety-Nines, 34, 38, 167, 169
Iowa
  Red Oak, 29
Ireland, 149, 153, 165
Italian
  campaign, 136
  Front, 136
Italy, 137-139
  Cesenatico, 140

— J —
James
  Betty (Teresa's sister), 7, 19, 28-30, 92
  Catherine (Teresa's sister), 19
  Francis X. (Teresa's brother), 1-2, 7
  Jack (Teresa's brother), 7, 19
  Teresa, viii-ix, xi-xii, 1-32, 35, 39-40, 44-51, 53-55,
    57-63, 66-67, 71, 76-104, 106-109, 111-117,
    119-127, 130-132, 134-136, 138, 141-153, 156-159,
    161-174, 177
Japanese, 34, 48-49, 51, 136
Jefferson Barracks National Cemetery, 146
Jeppesen (map), 103
Johnson, Dorothea, 72
Johnston, Colonel Henry R., 80
Johnston Airport (Pennsylvania), 16, 19, 27
Jones, Lieutenant, 88
Jordan, Lieutenant Richard H., 52, 55, 128
Jowell, Virgie, 157
Junior Commandos, 86

— K —
Kansas
  Atchison, 167
Kentucky
  Danville, 140
Kuntz, Opal Logan, 34

— L —
Labrador
  Goose Bay, 69
Lawler, Pat, 108
Lawrence College, Sarah, 48
LeGoff, Mr., 152
Lewis, Ted, 95
Link Company, 103
Link instrument trainer, 43
Lockheed plant, 129
Loker, William, 19
Long
  Frank, 98
  Mitchell, 159
Look, 81
Louisiana
  New Orleans, 86-87
  Shreveport, 90
Love, Nancy Harkness, 33, 35-41, 46, 52-53, 55, 61, 63,
  68-69, 72, 157-158, 162-163
Lundy, Liz, 58, 85-86, 107-108, 159
l'Union Francaise des Associations de Combattants de
  Joinville-le-Pont, 148

— M —
Mackey
  Joe, 15
  Marion, 65
Manchuria, 51
Mantz, Paul, 92-93, 95
Marcher, Mr., 132
Marsden, Doc, 21
Martin
  Colonel John F., 138
  George L. "Dink," xii, 19, 24, 27, 28, 29, 30, 44,
    141-144, 146-147, 149-152, 161, 167
  Lieutenant John E., 137
  Mrs. (George's mother), 24, 29-30
  Teresa (George's wife), *see* James, Teresa
  Virginia Clair "Tex," 85, 107
Martin bomber plant (Maryland), 37

Maryland
  Aberdeen, 115-116
  Baltimore, 37, 57, 70, 123
  Chesapeake Bay, 120
  Hagerstown, 62, 77-78, 80, 89, 92-93, 104, 125
Massachusetts
  Boston, 55, 64
  Orange, 64
Matz, Captain Onas P., 55, 80, 86
Maxwell Air Force Base (Alabama), xii
May, A. J., 162
Maytag Messerschmitt training, 59
McClintock Air Service, 32
McCormick
  Alma Heflin, 39
  Jill, 94, 157, 162
McCray, Neil, 71
McDarment, Captain Corley P., 15
McDowell, Natan M., 19
McGilvery, Helen, 39, 57, 63, 157-158
McGovern, Lieutenant James, 140
Means, Private D. I., 30
Mediterranean theater, 137-138
Melody, Captain, 171-172
Merchant Marine, 155
Michigan
  Detroit, 1, 55
  Houghton, 35
  Romulus, 42
  Romulus AAB, 61
Miller (Watson), Florene, 39, 55, 62, 66, 90
Mills, Irving, 97
Milton Academy (Massachusetts), 35
Mississippi
  Biloxi, 28
    Keesler Field, 28
  Jackson, 88, 91
  Jacksonville, 164
  McComb, 87
  Meridian, 88
  Selma, 88
Missouri
  Springfield, 107
  St. Louis, 2-3, 107, 146
Mitchell, General Billy, 48
Missing In Action, 142
Mogey, Gordon, 15
Monahan, Rita, 108
Montana
  Billings, 90
  Great Falls, 90-91, 115, 130
Monty's Pets, see 79th Fighter Group
Morse code, 52
Mosquito Fighter Group, see 79th Fighter Group
Motor Square Garden marathon, 8
Mountbatten, Lord Louis, 173
Moynahan, Rita, 157
Municipal Airport (Louisiana), 87

— N —
National Air and Space Museum, 168
National Mail Week, 19
Naval Air Station, 122
Navy Airport (Louisiana), 87
Nazis, 144
Nelson, Esther, 39-40, 48, 56-57, 78, 107
Neumann, Harold, 15
Neutrality Act, 37

Nevada
  Las Vegas, 90
Newark Airport, 136
Newark Army Air Base (New Jersey), 117, 135
New Castle Army Air Base (Delaware), xi, 38, 45-46,
    48-50, 52, 56, 58-59, 61, 64, 77, 79-80, 86, 99, 102,
    104, 111, 114-115, 123, 141, 143, 156, 167-169
Newcastle County Airport, 31, 79, 168
New England, 36
Newfoundland
  Gander, 36
New Hampshire
  Concord, 64
New Jersey, 83, 141
  Englewood, 46, 129
  Grantwood, 65
  Newark, 118, 123, 131
New Mexico
  Alamagordo, 72
  Albuquerque, 90
  Roswell, 141
New York, 15, 20, 24, 46, 83, 105, 134, 142, 146
  Long Island, 25, 27, 81, 84-85, 104, 106-108, 111-112,
      118, 123, 127, 131, 133
    Farmingdale, 131-133, 135, 142
    Huntington, 85-86, 145
      Huntington Hotel, 26, 84, 145
    Roosevelt Field, 25
    Syosset, 38
  New York City, 65, 83, 86
    Broadway, 83
    Radio City, 83
    Rainbow Room, 83
    The Slop Joint, 85
  Niagra Falls, 128
  Scarsdale, 65
New York Daily News, 144
Ninety-Nines, see International Organization of Women
    Pilots
Nixon
  Pat, (wife), 165
  Vice President Richard, 164
Normandy, 141
North Carolina
  Charlotte, 88, 92
  Wilmington, 126
Northern Italian campaign, 136
NOS (National Oceanic Survey), 103
Nutt, Marianne Beard, 132, 157, 159, 162

— O —
Oates, Eunice, 157
Oath of Allegiance, 19
Odlum, Floyd, 34
Officers Club, 46
Officers Training School, 165
  Ohio, 15
  Cincinnati, 39, 61
  Cleveland, 10, 95, 163
  Columbus, 107
  Dayton, 168
Oklahoma, 103-104, 115
Olds, General Robert, 35, 38
Olek Shipyards, Martin, 32
Olmstead Air Base (Pennsylvania), 37, 88
Operations Order, 80
Order of Fifinella, 168
OX-5 Association, 168

— P —

P-47 Pilots' Club, 131
P-47 Thunderbolt Pilots Association, xi, 147, 168
Pacific theater, 64, 72
Palm Beach International Airport, 167
Parks Air College (Missouri), 2-3
Parsons, Louella, 98
Patterson, Robert P., 134
Patuxent Naval Air Station, 120-121
Pearce
    Liz, 84, 132
    Sarah, 157
Penn Central Airline, 23
Pennsylvania, 15, 55
    Allegheny County, 15, 125
    Allentown, 83
    Blackridge, 2
    Clarion, 13-14
    Connellsville, 4
    Dravosburg, 19
    Duquesne Gardens, 8
    Erie, 71
    Harrisburg, 37
    Johnstown, 4
    Latrobe, 2
    Lock Haven, 81, 86, 88-89, 103
        Fallon Hotel, 88
    McKeesport, 125
    Middletown, 77, 88-89
    Penn Water Tower, 6
    Philadelphia, 88
    Pitcairn, 16, 19
    Pittsburgh, xi, 1, 7-8, 15-17, 23, 27, 30, 32, 44, 47,
        104, 142, 144, 164, 166, 172
        Aero Club, 16
        Fliers Club, 15
        Fort Pitt Hotel, 7
        Penn Hills, 8
        St. Paul's Cathedral, 8
    Scranton, 77
    Titusville, 67
    Turtle Creek, 24, 29
    Wilkinsburg, 4, 8, 11, 19, 21, 131, 163
        High School, 8
        Post Office, 18
Pennsylvania Air Station, 120-121
Pennsylvania Skating Association, 8
Philadelphia Evening Bulletin, 41
Pierced steel planking (PSP), 88
Pinkley, Avanell, 157, 162
Pinkston, Colonel Gladwyn E., 136
Piper factory, 81
Pitz, Josephine "Jo," 85, 106-107, 157
Poole
    Barbara, 39, 55, 88, 162
    Esther, 157
POW, 144
Primary Instructor Rating, 20
Primary training, 30, 42
Private License, 8, 35
Pullman, 88
Pursuit School, 64
Pyhota, Bill, 25-26
Pyle, Ernie, 126, 143
PX, 43

— R —

Racers, 131, 134

RADAR, 61
RAF, 147
Rappaport, Max, 25-27
Rathfelder (Westervelt), Esther, 39, 162
Ravenna, 138
Rawls
    Captain Theodore H., 64
    Katherine Thompson (Theodore's wife), 41, 62, 64,
        66, 90
Ray, Maggie, 157
Red Cross, 41, 86
Red Letter Day, 79
Republic Aviation Corporation, 104-105, 126, 132-135,
    137, 142
Republic Aviation factory, ix, xi, 85, 107-108, 111, 131,
    133, 135, 159
Republic Farmingdale Division, 134
Rhineland, 141
Rhonie, Aline, 39-41, 46
Richards (Prosser), Helen, 39, 55, 67, 88
Richey, Helen, 23, 84-85, 107, 124-126, 132, 143, 157,
    159
Rio Grande, 69
Rising Sun, 48
Ritter, Tex, 164, 173
Robinson, Bojangles, 97
Rodgers civilian airport, John (Hawaii), 48
Roma, 138
RON (remained overnight), 89, 91
Rosenbloom, Sergeant, 106, 118, 120
Roosevelt
    Eleanor, 34
    Franklin D., Jr., 27
    President Franklin D., 19, 64
Roosevelt Field (New York), 41
Roosevelt School of Aviation, 12
Ross, Barney, 97-98
Ross Corps, Betsy, 34
Rothschild, Baron, 98
Royal Air Force Club, 173
R/T (radio telephone), 125
Russia, 130, 155
Russo, Mary, 157
Ryan Aeronautical Company, 39

— S —

Saccio, Lieutenant, 46, 77
Santa Maria, 30
Secondary Instructor's Rating, 24
Scharr, Adela (Del) "Madame P-Shooter," 39-40, 49,
    83, 127, 129-130
Scott, Dorothy, 41
Scottish, 34
Service Forces, 155
Sharp, Evelyn, 41, 78
Sicilian campaign, 136
Silver Wings Association, 168
Simms, Ginny, 95, 98
Slocum
    Catherine, 39-41
    Richard W. (Catherine's husband), 41
Smithsonian Institute, The, 54, 168
Snafu (situation normal, all fouled up Airlines), 122-123
South Carolina, 130
    Spartanburg, 88
South Plains Army Air Field (Texas), 69
Soviet Union, 130
Starbuck, Lieutenant, 77

Stimson, Henry L., 37
Stockton Field, 144
Stormy Weather, 97
Straughn, Jane, 65, 157
Stunt pilot, xi, 8-9, 12, 15-16, 21, 30

— T —

Tache, Magda, 65, 162
Tennessee, 89
  Jackson, 67, 90
  Memphis, 27, 90
    Ferrying Division, 27
  Nashville, 89
Texas, 44, 55, 64, 115, 129
  Abilene, 43, 113
  Amarillo, 67, 90
  Brownsville, 64, 130
  Dallas, 42, 56, 90, 114
    Love Field, 61
  Dallas AAB, 61
  El Paso, 113
  Houston, 41-43, 113, 163
  Lubbock, 69
  Midland, 113
  Odessa, 67
  Sweetwater, 41-43, 72
  Wichita Falls, 62, 90
    Sheppard Field, 62
Thaden, Louise, 34
Tibbets, Paul W., 71-72
Tomak Aviation Corporation, 30-32
Tomak, Bill, 30
Towne (Fasken), Barbara, 41, 67, 88
TR (Transportation Request), 87
Tracy
  Lieutenant Joe, 77, 132
  Spencer, 95
Transport License, xi, 38
Tricycle landing gear, 35
Triest, Lieutenant, 88
Tubbs, Gertrude Meserve, 39, 55, 57-58, 63-65, 85-86,
  104-110, 117, 122-124, 132, 158-159, 162
Tulane, 87
Tunisian campaign, 136
Tunner, Colonel, 64, 69
Turner, Roscoe, 19

— U —

Uncle Sam, 44
United States, ix, 19, 34, 38, 49, 52, 73, 75, 92, 126,
  136, 149, 155
U.S., ix, 25, 27, 34-35, 41, 69
  Air Guard, 138
  Air Force Active Reserve, 164
  Army, 2, 16, 19, 25, 27-29, 37-38, 41, 44, 52, 55,
    76-77, 79, 83, 91-92, 120-121, 124, 126, 129, 131,
    134, 138, 144-145, 163, 165, 174-176
  Army Air Corps, 15, 34, 42, 53
  Army Air Forces, ix, xi, 23, 31, 35, 37-38, 41, 48, 53,
    68-69, 72, 74, 76, 79, 115, 125, 130-131, 136-137,
    144-146, 153-155, 161, 169
  Air Force Reserve, xi, 39, 171, 174
  Mail, 17, 19
  Marines, 88-89, 97
  Military Affairs Committee, 72
  Navy, 39, 64, 94, 121, 155
  War Department, 34, 38, 134, 153

— V —

Vassar College, 33, 35
Veterans Administration, 75
Veterans Association, 146, 149
Veterans of Foreign Wars, 16
  Morrison Robinson Post, 16
VFR (Visual Flight Rules), 61, 88
Vietnam, 103, 163
Virginia
  Alexandria, 65
  Charlottesville, 88
  Culpeper, 137-138
  Danville, 88, 128
  Lynchburg, 92
  Quantico, 88-89
VOC (Visiting Officers Quarters), 88
Vogue, 48

— W —

Wake Island, 88
Walker, C. I., 102
Warner Brothers, 98
Washington
  Seattle, 55, 114
Washington, D.C., 37, 41, 44, 65, 72, 91, 144, 168
WASP wings, 68
Weiss, Margaret, 68
Wertheimer, Pfc. George, 145
Westinghouse plant, 19
West Point Military Academy, 89
"Widow Maker," *see* B-26
Wilkes, Rita, 128
Wilkinsburg Airport (Pennsylvania), xi, 1, 6-8, 11-12,
  18, 21
Williams Air Force Base (Arizona), 59
Wilmington Warriors, 80
Winters, Bob, 28
Witsell, Major General Edward, 146
Wolf, Philip J., 146
Women Airforce Service Pilots (WASP), ix, xi, 43, 54,
  68-75, 89, 125, 131, 134, 138, 143-144, 147, 154-156,
  160-161, 163, 165, 167, 174
Women's Air Reserve, 34
Women's Auxiliary Ferrying Squadron (WAFS), xi, 33,
  37-41, 43-44, 46, 48, 52-57, 59-61, 64-65, 67-69, 72,
  76-77, 79-83, 86, 88, 92, 95-96, 99, 102, 111, 129,
  130, 154, 164, 167-169, 174-175, 177
Women's Flying Training Detachment (WFTD), 41-44,
  64-65, 68
World War I, 19, 45
World War II, ix, xi, 19, 34, 75, 80, 146-147, 153,
  166-167
Wuest, Lieutenant Harold, 140
Wyoming
  Casper, 90

— Y —

Yocum, William P., 18
Young, Dorothy, 65

— Z —

Zoot suits, 43
Zuchowski, Janet, 128, 157